Historical role analysis in the study of religious change

This study in historical sociology explores the relationship between educational development and religious change in Norwegian society during a period of significant social and economic transition. John Flint traces the process whereby the laity radically reduced clerical control over religious institutions. In contrast to the usual preoccupation with sectarian movements, this book focuses upon religious protest movements which *remained within* the established order and shows how they were an integral part of a general trend towards the dissolution of religious unity.

The author examines census materials, reports to the Ministry of the Church and Education, and quantifiable information contained in organizational histories – using historical role analysis to describe the changing relationship between state church pastors, parish school teachers, pupils, parents, and lay preachers.

With these materials, his study draws on and contributes to the sociology of comparative educational development, in an examination of the movement towards mass literacy. Professor Flint's account of religious protest movements analyzes their emergence as related to the processes whereby popular literacy was increased, which facilitated religious mobilization among the laity. The conclusions he draws from this Norwegian study have wider theoretical and methodological implications, and will be of interest to historians and those studying the sociology of religion and education.

For other titles in the series, please turn to the end of this volume.

Historical role analysis in the study of religious change

Mass educational development in Norway, 1740–1891

John T. Flint
Department of Sociology
State University of New York at Binghamton

Cambridge University Press
Cambridge
New York   Port Chester
Melbourne   Sydney

Published by the Press Syndicate of the University of Cambridge
The Pitt Building, Trumpington Street, Cambridge CB2 1RP
40 West 20th Street, New York, NY 10011, USA
10 Stamford Road, Oakleigh, Melbourne 3166, Australia

First published 1990

Printed in Great Britain at the University Press, Cambridge

British Library cataloguing in publication data

Flint, John T.
Historical role analysis in the study of religious change: mass educational development
in Norway, 1740–1891. – (The Arnold and Caroline Rose monograph series of the
American Sociological Association). 1. Norway. Religion. Sociological perspectives,
1740–1900.
I. Title   II. Series
306'.6'09481

Library of Congress cataloguing in publication data applied for

ISBN 0 521 37099 X

VN

Contents

Tables

Preface

The border between historical sociology and social history has become so permeable in recent years as to be nonexistent for a growing number of practitioners. Nevertheless, it is probably true that most social historians make little if any effort to test or extract *explicit* propositions of a more general explanatory character. Their emphasis continues to be upon making intelligible a particular sequence of social acts and relationships with reference to some aspects of a specified time period and location. Propositions and generalizations may be more or less *implicit* in the guise of research questions which define and guide selective criteria in terms of which a monograph is prepared. Among many historical sociologists, more or less explicit conceptual schemes adapted from earlier research on a similar range of social phenomena are often utilized as central elements defining the major variables of testable propositions which may be confirmed, rejected, or modified by the new case material.[1]

The ambivalence I experienced in trying to decide upon a reasonably accurate title for this book may serve to illustrate the ambiguities of these rather blurred distinctions. My first but not ultimate choice, "Mass educational development and popular religious change in preindustrial Norway, 1740–1891," provided a straightforward indication of time, place, and social historical topic. My primary concerns, however, are more general in a substantive and methodological sense. Thus, my final title became as it now reads, "Historical role analysis in the study of religious change," sub-title, "Mass educational development in Norway, 1740–1891." This comes much closer to expressing my historical–sociological objectives.

I have sought to address the concerns of those scholars interested in the scientific study of popular religious change. Perhaps my most distinctive contribution to the literature will consist of a focus upon those much-neglected religious protest movements which *remain within* an established order in contrast to the much more familiar preoccupation with sectarian movements. The latter are included but receive secondary emphasis. Interwoven with these foci is considerable systematic attention to the process of secularization as part of a general trend toward the dissolution of religious unity, of which the protests are also an integral part.

Secondly, I have drawn upon and attempted to contribute something to the sociology of comparative educational development, with particular focus upon the social organization of mass literacy production as this impinged upon the religious mobilization of a laity in a preindustrial context.

Finally, regional historical variations in systems of social stratification provide the comparative context within which descriptions of the interplay between mass educational developments and popular religious change are presented and partial explanatory sketches constructed.[2] Throughout the text I have tried to utilize what I label "historical role analysis" as a device for structuring the descriptive process, focusing above all upon the changing relationships between state-church pastors, parish school teachers, pupils, parents, and lay preachers.

Where possible, I have drawn upon official records (census reports, reports to the Ministry of Church and Education, etc.) or secondary analysis of quantifiable materials contained in organizational histories in order to sharpen comparative descriptions of educational systems at the diocesan and provincial levels as well as similar regional variations in the timing, tempo, and magnitude of popular religious mobilization, particularly between 1860 and 1891.

Most of the above could be translated into the more formal language of conventional sociological analysis – for example, dependent (religious mobilization), independent (educational role-system development), and contingent (class analytic) variables. Such statements of relationship (propositions) probably could be "derived" from an integrated codification of what passes for theory in the sociology of religious movements, secularization, and educational development. Such an effort, while possibly of value in another context, would, I believe, tend to obscure some of my more modest objectives and at the same time misrepresent my own evolving skepticism regarding the adequacy of timeless and spaceless claims of some varieties of structural/functional as well as conflict theory. It is my contention that historical role analysis is a procedural, descriptive device which may be congruent with, accessible to, and translatable into a variety of alternative, though not necessarily mutually exclusive, interpretive perspectives. In short, it is my hope that I have provided grist for several alternative theoretical mills, not excluding my own reconsiderations at some later time.

Part of the reason for this rather cautious approach to explanatory claims derives from the relative absence of a long-term controversial literature within Norwegian historiography of a kind comparable in depth and scope to that in England on, for example, the cause, course, and consequences of the Puritan

Revolution (or Civil War?), or the Halevey thesis regarding the counter-revolutionary functions of the Methodist Movement.[3] Obviously, as I note below, without the superb work of Molland, Mannsaaker, and Dokka, as well as of Stein Rokkan, Vilhelm Aubert, and the research associates of the last two, this enterprise never would have been undertaken. It is not that controversies relevant to my concerns here have not been evident. For example, the scope and impact of the Hauge movement, as well as patterns of political mobilization and conflict after about 1869, have certainly generated scholarly controversy, but not, in my view, of the often radically divergent variety so familiar among English social historians. Such controversies not only sharpen perspectives but often generate a wider range of empirical research which thus becomes available to later interpreters with still other axes to grind. The relevance of all this will, I trust, become evident throughout the text, particularly with reference to changing patterns of class, status, and power as between major regions between 1740 and 1891 where I have built upon the work of Skappel, Steen, Semmingsen, Mannsaaker, Rokkan, and Aubert. The unresolved ambiguities of this social–historical process are grappled with most directly in chapter 5.

One of the pleasures of social research comes in learning how generous many people can be in facilitating that process. During the initial phase of my work this included the staff of the University Library in Oslo, the Norwegian Central Statistical Bureau, the Royal Archive, and the church history section of the library at the University Theological Faculty, as well as the Institute for Pedagogy. The Institute for Social Research was most hospitable in providing work space during a summer research period in Oslo. On my return to Binghamton, two centers became absolutely indispensable to my efforts: first that glorious treasure trove, the New York Public Library, and secondly the interlibrary loan section of the SUNY/Binghamton Library, particularly during the periods when Janet Brown, Rochelle Moore, and Nancy Huling were in charge. My special appreciation goes to Gloria Gaumer, Lisa Fegley-Schmidt, and their staff at the manuscript center for typing the several drafts of this work. Nancy Hall and Nettie Rathje in the Sociology Department were most helpful in ways too numerous and diverse to be listed here. Finally, my thanks go to the University Awards Program of the State University of New York for providing a grant making possible a research summer in Oslo which laid part of the foundation for later work.

My scholarly indebtedness to Dagfinn Mannsaaker, Hans Jørgen Dokka, and the late Einar Molland will become evident to the reader. Dr. Mann-saaker, one-time Royal Archivist and editor of *Historisk Tidsskrift* and, above all, distinguished social historian of Norwegian religious life in the nineteenth century, must be acknowledged as the single most helpful guide to bibliographic sources. He also made me aware of the network of scholars most relevant to my concerns. Professor Dokka is a case in point. He expanded my awareness of the then (1969) available secondary literature on the history of the several levels of Norway's educational system as well as some more crucial gaps and limitations of that literature.

Erling Reksten and Ulf Torgersen of Oslo University's history and political science faculties respectively provided additional guidance and, above all, together with Thomas Mathiesen of the law faculty, provided a rich and warm personal, conversational context which I will always remember as among the most stimulating of my professional life. Erik Rinde, founding director and long-term patron of the Institute for Social Research whose generous hospitality greatly facilitated my work, was part of that context.

My long-time friend and fellow student of things Scandinavian, Mari Lund Wright, responded promptly and generously to several requests for needed materials. Most particularly, she brought me in contact, indirectly, with the late Ola Rudvin through her correspondence with him, which enabled me to clarify, if only in part, certain problems of interpretation of his text, used extensively in chapter 3 below.

The most extensive critiques of the manuscript I owe to the generosity of Professors Robin Williams, Charles Tilley, Robert Wuthnow, and Henry Valen, the latter of the University of Oslo and a major contributor to the historical–ecological study of political change in Norway. The three readers for the Arnold Rose Monograph Series, then anonymous, now acknowledged elsewhere, helped me to sharpen the argument, and cautioned me against assuming too much about a potential reader's knowledge of the history of a small country on the European scholarly periphery. Professor Ernest Q. Campbell, editor of the series, focused my attention on the most salient features of those critiques and thus facilitated my efforts to respond to their recommendations. Finally, Wendy Guise and Charles W. Hieatt, general and copy-editor, respectively, at Cambridge University Press, provided the most tangible assistance of all. Dr. Hieatt's meticulous attention to the language of the text brought my attention to some of its ambiguities I was simply too blind to see.

Among my professional colleagues at SUNY-Binghamton who have read and commented upon it in whole or in part are John Casparis, Ronald Fullerton, James Geschwender, Melvin Leiman, and Dag Tangen, a visiting scholar from Oslo University. It is, of course, my hope that by including the several modifications and additions suggested, the quality and readability of the manuscript have been significantly enhanced. As usual, the remaining weaknesses in the text are my own invention and responsibility.

Three persons must be mentioned who share a rather different relationship to my efforts. My teacher and friend, the late Hans Gerth, provided a model of erudition, of intellectual passion and excitement which remains one part of my inner life as a scholar. It is, to be sure, a part of me which also delayed completion of the manuscript. Professor Sylvia Thrupp, founding editor of *Comparative Studies in Society and History*, someone I have met only through her generous and immensely helpful correspondence in connection with articles for her journal, provided a kind of encouragement which is the salvation of many a discouraged young would-be professional. The present book, only one chapter of which she saw in an early draft, is significantly linked to that moral support. Finally, my dear wife, Frieda, who has had to live with a rather short manuscript for a very long time, and whose editorial preference for at least a few short sentences greatly improved the readability of the text – to her I owe more than the traditional debt.

Note on Norwegian place names

Throughout the text, statistical tables, and in the outline map showing provincial and diocesan boundaries, I have used twentieth-century names rather than those to be found in official reports (census, etc.) of all sorts throughout the nineteenth century and earlier. The similarities and differences can be indicated as follows, with the earlier names in parentheses. *Provinces:* Akershus (Akershus), Østfold (Smaalene), Vestfold (Jarlsberg og Laurvig), Buskerud (Buskerud), Hedmark (Hedmarken), Oppland (Kristians), Telemark (Bratsberg), Aust-Agder (Nedenes), Vest-Agder (Lister og Mandal), Rogaland (Stavanger), Hordaland (Søndre Bergenshus), Sogn og Fjordane (Nordre Bergensus), Møre og Romsdal (Romsdal), Sør-Trondelag (Søndre Trondhjem), Nord-Trondelag (Nordre Trondhjem), Nordland (Nordland), Troms (Tromsø), Finmark (Finmarken). *Dioceses:* Oslo (Kristiania), Hamar (Hamar), Kristiansand (Agder), Bergen (Bergen), Trondhjem (Trondhjem), Tromsø (Tromsø).

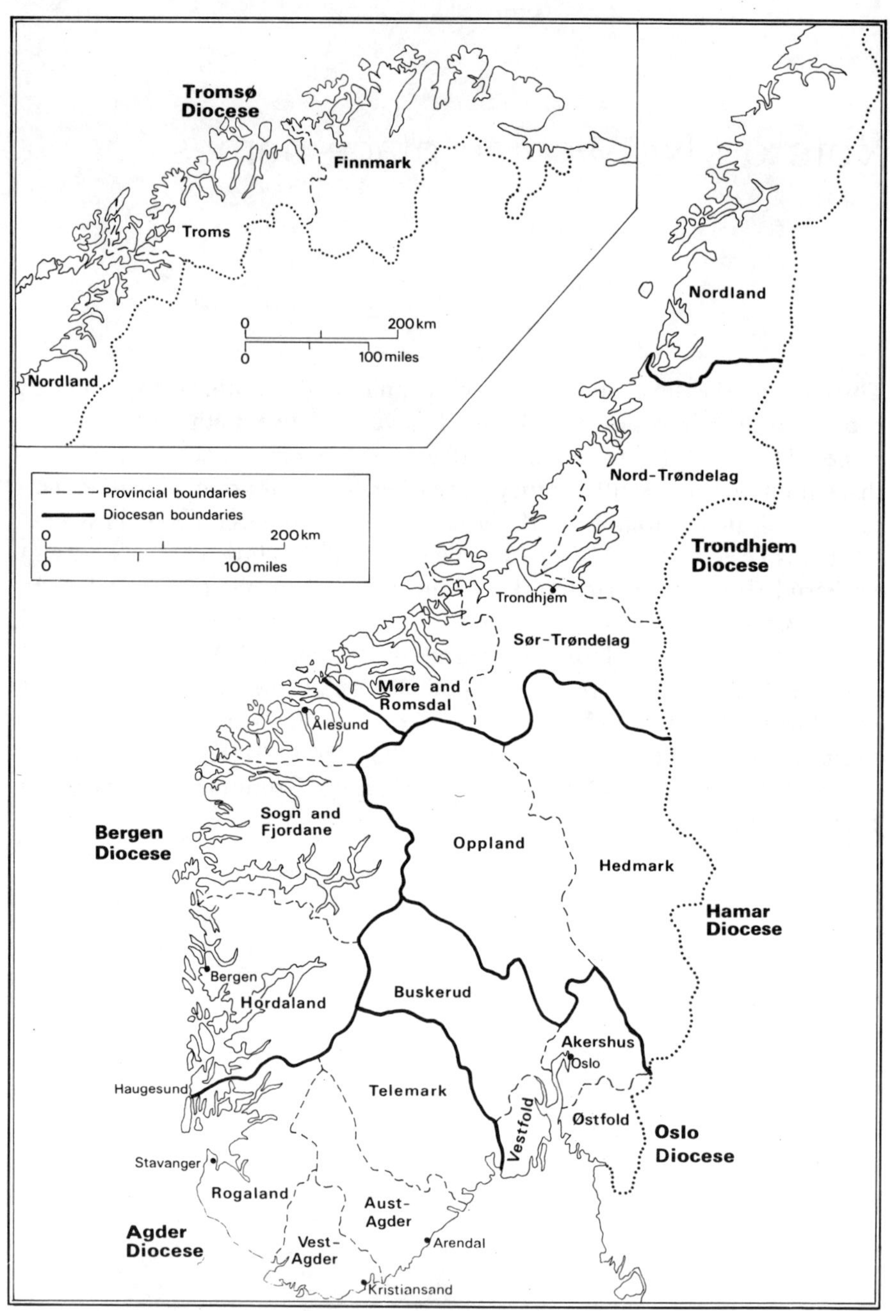

Provinces and dioceses of Norway, c. 1865, using twentieth-century place names

1. Introduction

A concern with the prerequisites for and consequences of mass educational development has been a recurrent theme in both the history and historiography of those societies where knowledge and skills based on literacy were regarded as preconditions for power and economic growth. Systematic comparative study of this interplay has been devoted in large measure to educational correlates of nation-building and economic growth since 1950.[1] Economic historians and others have drawn renewed attention to a similar range of phenomena in the preindustrial West and Japan.[2]

Partial explanations for the differential timing and tempo of mass as opposed to elite literacy diffusion in preindustrial settings have been constructed from variations in the content and articulation of role, ritual, and belief systems within and between the major world religions. Thus, Western religions of The Book have, in principle, been more conducive to mass literacy than Eastern religions of The Way. Egalitarian organization combined with inner-worldly life orientations produced a literate laity well before reading skills were required by new technologies or an expanding electorate.[3] Where less egalitarian modes of religious role organization prevailed, as in the state churches of Germany and Scandinavia, popular education was promoted, initially, by laicized or lay-oriented varieties of Lutheran pietism in tension with Orthodox clericalism as part of absolutist styles of administration.

Once initiated in these more authoritarian systems, religious literacy exposed the lower and middle strata of the laity to a range of hitherto less accessible symbolic resources which provided one of the preconditions for (1) altered definitions of religiosity, (2) the progressive laicization of religious life, and (3) incipient secularization.

Social-historical analyses of this interplay between educational development and religious change based on broadly representative evidence describing one or more dimensions of the two sets of variables directly involved are, to my knowledge, nonexistent. Given the relationship between historical visibility of a stratum and its location in any system of power and privilege, it is hardly surprising that generalizations regarding this relationship are most persuasive at elite levels. That is to say, as we move from higher to lower levels of educational experience, from elite to more popular styles of religiosity, the scope and depth of our evidence is reduced. Norway provides one example of a very small number of nation-state with a rather long history of central statistical record-keeping, not only of a general demographic nature but also extensive data relevant to these phenomena at a popular level.

It is my objective in this book to explore some procedural and substantive problems encountered in the study of mass educational development and popular religious change in Norwegian society between 1740 and 1891. This effort seeks to be of some value in clarifying the comparative study of that broad class of social-historical phenomena in other preindustrial contexts.

Let us begin with a series of statements designed to link this research focus to a more general set of conceptual/analytic perspectives.[4] First, by "social-change analysis" I refer to the comparative study of classes of social-historical phenomena ranging in levels of abstraction from the interpersonal act to world systems. This descriptive activity seeks to formulate and/or test propositions or systems of logically related propositions which hope to predict and/or explain whatever class of phenomena is under consideration. Such an effort requires a system of more or less explicit interrelated concepts which organize the descriptive process, whether comparative or not. I have found the following conceptual scheme helpful as adapted from the work of Hans Gerth and C. Wright Mills, *Character and Social Structure*, incorporating some elements from Peter Berger's *The Sacred Canopy*, and extending both by including my rather primitive version of Immanuel Wallerstein's world-systems theory. All of these I find congruent with my own symbolic interactionist and structural orientation.

By the "interpersonal act" I refer to a system of symbols composing a norm which limits and defines a particular unit of other-oriented conduct. By their recurrence, these acts stand out as regularities and constitute the *social role* level of description as in Merton's role sets and tasks. My descriptive focus is largely at this level, so much so that I considered entitling this book, "Pastors, preachers, pupils, and teachers within a preindustrial society." These roles are enacted within *institutional* settings: that is, "organizations of roles one or more of which is an authority role." Once again, we will be tracing shifting distributions of authority within and between parishes, dioceses, and school districts, as well as patterns of authority within lay movements from local to regional to national levels of institutionalization. Historians, anthropologists, sociologists, and others, whatever their several differences may be, tend to share a classification of institutions according to their objective functions or ends, whether untended or inintended, into a minimum of four major clusters:

political, economic, religious, and kinship. These clusters I will refer to as "institutional orders," which vary over time in terms of their internal diversity as well as the mode and degree of *interplay* between those more or less diverse institutions classified within the order. A major reason for selecting the Norwegian case was precisely the relatively high level of homogeneity within its religious order even into the twentieth century, in contrast to the much-studied, long-term pluralism of the United States, Britain, Holland, Belgium, and other western European religious orders which have constituted almost but not quite totally the empirical base for "theory construction" in the sociology of religious change during the past fifty years or so.

Until the explicit, very self-conscious appearance of world-systems theory, the most abstract unit of comparative descriptive study and theory formation was the nation-state, political economy, society, or, in the vocabulary to which I have grown accustomed, "social structure." The present book was prepared as part of a long-term interest in viewing Norway as a system of interrelated institutional orders with varying modes and degrees of integration from tenth-century paganism to the immensely greater range of symbolic resources and orientations of twentieth-century life within an effective world system of vast ideological variations. General reflections about the existence of a world system regarded as a system of interrelated social structures with varying modes and degrees of interdependence from one historical situation to another is hardly a product of the last twenty years. However, the self-conscious, explicit conceptual refinements and theoretical disputations generated by this perspective linked to systematic empirical evidence are usually regarded as of rather recent vintage.[5] Except for the efforts of Robert Wuthnow, I am not aware of any concerted attempt to re-examine the social history of religions within this framework.[6] Any history of the religious order in Norwegian social structure from paganism to socialism could hardly ignore Norway's obvious "dependence" on external sources of symbolic input at every major point of internal religious transformation, from the alleged eleventh-century conversion to the vagaries of twentieth-century multi-dimensional symbolic worlds with sacred elements persisting in an allegedly secular world. I will return to my use of the word "alleged" below, as related to some long-term controversies concerning the concept of secularization.

The transmission of religious heritages from generation to generation through a continuing process of socialization has usually been regarded as a human universal. By definition, this process occurs at the interpersonal level via those social actions, "formal and informal," whereby symbols and skills are transmitted to those who do not already possess them and are continually reinforced and/or modified through a life-long dialectic in which our social worlds are thought to be constructed, sustained, and transformed.[7] Given the fact that, even as I write, current sociologists of education, whether of religious symbol systems or otherwise, with their access to immediately observable data, remain understandably cautious regarding bland certainties about the outcome of these actions, and the limitations of historical sociologists hardly deserve explicit reference.

It is precisely for this reason, acknowledged or otherwise, that social historians have tended to locate their most micro-level descriptions at the role level of abstraction. In this sense virtually all social-historical description is based on a tissue of assumptions and inferences informed, implicitly or explicitly, by an analytic/descriptive strategy.

Granted these very general considerations and caveats, let us return somewhat closer to the task at hand, after a deliberately brief consideration of how I will be using the words "religion," "religious order," and "secularization" insofar as this is not self-evident in the main body of my exposition. The current chaotic state of so-called secularization theory[8] prompts me to adopt a "Humpty-Dumpty" approach to these problems of definition: that is, to paraphrase, "when I use these words this is what I will mean by them, neither more nor less." First, to those readers with functionalist preferences I offer the following modification of Lenski's version of Durkheim.[9] By "religion" I refer to any system of beliefs about the nature of the force or forces which ultimately shape the destiny of man, and the ritual system associated therewith shared by the members of a role system. This formulation, which is intended to have highly generalized relevance, contains structural elements with functionalist presuppositions. Since it is my view that definitions are useful or not useful (rather than true or false) in a particular research context, I prefer for present purposes a culturally limited structural definition in line with my general conceptual scheme outlined above. That is, a "religious order" is composed of those institutions within which people worship God or Gods, usually at regular times and at fixed places.[10] The many specific religious orders which have existed, coexisted, or do exist within particular social structures in time and space are empirically distinguishable on two major interrelated dimensions: (a) in the context and articulation of their three major components, i.e., their belief, ritual, and role systems, and (b) in their relationship with consequences for other institutional orders within their social structures. Finally, by "secularization" in this conceptual language I will be referring to the decline and even "disappearance" of a historically specific religious order as an independent and/or contingent variable in social conduct, process, and change.

It would seem to follow from this limited structural definition that the alleged displacement of Norwegian paganism by a certain variety of Medieval Catholicism (i.e., Cluniac) was in turn reformed out of existence by a series of distinguishable Lutheran belief systems which are now said to be fading away into who knows how many varieties of implicit, invisible, civil, or other public and/or private belief systems, each of which phenomena may be regarded as an example of religious change (in general) and secularization in particular. Well, why not? It seems to me that much of the controversy over this concept – insofar as it has an empirical reference and has not simply been defined out of existence by some functionalist (motto: "Old religions never die, they differentiate") – derives from the almost total preoccupation with pluralistic societies after about 1945.

There is one critical point coming from functionalist quarters which I find relevant and challenging. That is the charge that the entire concept of secularization is anchored in an historical myth about an Age of Faith, whether Catholic (i.e., thirteenth century) or Protestant (*c.* 1525–?). My use of the words "alleged" and "allegedly" derive from this charge. After all, given the problems distinguished scholars like Robert Bellah and David Martin seem to have with the twentieth century, how can we talk persuasively about any period before the advent of George Gallup? If then? Given sufficiently rigorous empirical requirements we simply cannot do so.

I have rejected such criteria and have attempted to show how we might construct some broadly representative, indirect indicators of past religiosity without relying on pious anecdotes about historically visible personalities or those intoxicating intellectual–historical generalizations about Thomas Aquinas or Martin Luther as though the former's *Summa* or the latter's *Table Talk* demonstrates something about the religious experience of Portuguese peasants or Norwegian farmers. Whether I have made some modest progress in this direction must be left to the reader's judgment.

Leaving these unresolved controversies behind, let us return to the main line of the argument: namely, the social mechanisms whereby religious beliefs, rituals, and role were and are transmitted from one generation to another. The content, social organization, and outcome of this process, usually differentiated along lines of social stratification, are obviously highly variable both historically and across cultural systems. Among these variations is the extent to which knowledge of the belief system and ritual prerogatives is more or less monopolized by a body of specialists, in principle or in practice. Historically, definitions of what constitutes "true religiosity" within a given tradition have tended to be controlled by these specialists. Where knowledge of a sacred literature has been included among these criteria of religiosity, pressures toward some variety of popular literacy production have existed at least as a potential development. If this has issued in the rote memorization of a sacred text in a language other than the vernacular, it may be argued that both educational development, in the sense of functional literacy, and religious change have been more effectively inhibited.

One of the several distinctive and highly consequential outcomes of the Protestant Reformation derived precisely from the promotion of religious objectives via mass functional literacy in languages closer to, though by no means identical with, the vernacular(s). The creation of national languages out of regional dialects was at least partly the product of this religiously inspired educational process.

Protestantism, perhaps more than any other world religion, has been associated with two interrelated varieties of religious change: diversification and secularization. By the former term I refer to three major classes of phenomena. First, the proliferation of theologically distinct perspectives within a given religious order which may or may not take the form of a church "party" and are dominated by variable portions of the established clergy. Church of England Evangelicals, Apostolicals, and Latitudinarians as well as Orthodox, Pietist, and Rationalist varieties of German and Scandinavian Lutheranism represent historically discernible cases in point.[11]

Secondly, the laicization of religious initiative often associated with rising levels of doctrinal literacy and sensitivity has issued in a concomitant decline in clerical control over definitions of religiosity and altered role relationships within the established order. This class of phenomena has become historically visible in a variety of forms ranging from clerically guided lay activism to incipient sectarian movements which are ultimately reabsorbed in the established order through a process of more or less mutual cooptation.[12]

Finally, sectarian splits from the traditional system constitute the most clear-cut, dramatic, and studied of all forms of diversification by historical sociologists of religious change.[13] The other two are usually relegated to part of the generating context and seldom serve as the focus of systematic empirical description and explanatory concern.

The three varieties of diversification, including the sectarian, occur within a given social historical-religious tradition as broadly conceived. The concept of secularization, as I have indicated above, has been applied to a wide range of structural and symbolic phenomena which are thought to weaken and/or displace traditional religious conceptions, whether established, laicized, or sectarian.[14]

These forms of religious expression and change were conditioned by differential educational experiences. Among the more familiar empirical generalizations regarding these relationships are the following. First, it is almost tautological to observe that both the differentiation of clerical theologies and the secularization of upper-strata life orientations have been linked to changes within higher educational settings. For example, Norwegian church historians have attributed the sequence of five distinguishable clerical "generations" in the state church parishes between 1740 and 1891 to corresponding changes in theological formulations at the university training centers at Copenhagen and, after 1811, at Oslo. These in turn derived partially from reorientations in Lutheran theology at German universities. Access to more secular varieties of the continental and English Enlightenment was largely restricted to urban merchants in international trade and higher officials in the state bureaucracy, whose more extensive travel and varied educational experiences enhanced receptivity to such divergent ideas as part of their life style as a status group.

Historical and cross-national variations in the relationship between the social organization and content of mass literacy production and the diversification of popular religiosity have included two rather obvious general types. The religious pluralism of eighteenth- and nineteenth-century England and America was partially reflected in and reinforced by a fragmented range of educational agencies and opportunities. Norway, on the other hand, represents one case of those societies where initial religious uniformity was reflected in and reinforced by a highly integrated system of common school education.

As considerations of national identity and economic growth began to supplement religious objectives in the shaping of educational policy, particularly after 1814, corresponding changes occurred in the organization and content of mass educational experience. Given the differential starting points in pluralistic as opposed to unified systems, it seems reasonable to anticipate that the style and impact of such changes would vary accordingly. The following exploration in historical role analysis is intended as a contribution to the comparative study of this process by focusing attention where possible upon some regional contrasts in these two sets of interacting variables, primarily in rural Norwegian society between about 1740 and 1891.

The rationale underlying historical role analysis as a procedural alternative for the description and interpretation of religious change (e.g., diversification, secularization) may be summarized as follows.[15] The most commonly utilized indicators of religiosity are based upon selected aspects of belief or ritual systems. A third possibility relates to the role system dimension of religious orders. This system is the most immediate interpersonal context of ritual acts and beliefs of any religion. Sociologically, one can certainly argue, beliefs and rituals have no consequential significance unless they are institutionalized in role systems.

Assuming, then, that these three dimensions are interdependent, we may infer that a direct indicator of change in the role system may also be taken as an indirect indicator of change in one or both of the other two as well. Next, it is asserted that in all such systems, from the varieties of shamanism to styles of hierarchical priestly systems, there is a differential distribution of ritual skills and/or belief-system knowledge. Thus, while it is often asserted that Sunni, unlike Shiite, Islam is a religion without a laity since it lacks a priesthood, no scholar argues that Koranic knowledge is uniformly distributed throughout any population, as witness the Allamah, the Kadi, and other role labels in the world of Sunni Islam. Any religious order, then, can be described in terms of the role content of its "clergies" and laities. Further, as we will see in the Norwegian case, change in this system may occur in role tasks, sets, and/or power and prestige, reciprocally or independently. Finally, indicators of religious change, whether diversification or secularization, can be constructed in terms of specified kinds of transformations in that system.

Perhaps the most fundamental indicator for which data are often available to the historical sociologist is the ratio of laymen to clergymen. This ratio, depending on the problem at hand, may be taken as an indirect indicator of religiosity, as in studies of secularization or as providing quantitative evidence for one of several predisposing and/or inhibiting conditions for other types of religious diversification as well.

The internal or face validity of this ratio is based on the following refinements on the discussion thus far. (1) Where control over and knowledge of ritual skills and beliefs is restricted (*de jure* or *de facto*) to specialists, the ratio of lay population to such religious functionaries becomes one major factor in the maintenance of the traditional system. If such specialists decline in number relative to the laity for whom they are responsible, it follows that the frequency of clergy–laity contacts must also decline and the effective influence of the belief and ritual systems for which they are the prime carriers must also be weakened. (2) Logically, the validity of this ratio as an indicator of secularization varies directly with the extent to which a clergy monopolizes belief-system knowledge and ritual skills. This is, of course, an empirical variable cross-culturally and, as in the Norwegian case, historically. Thus, in Roman Catholicism where this monopoly is (or was), in principle, very high, relative to Islam, Judaism, or Protestant groups with congregational polities, this ratio would constitute a more valid indicator than it would for these other systems. (3) Finally, insofar as the allocation of land, labor, and capital among alternatives may be taken to reflect value preferences within a human society, the laity/clergy ratio provides a useful indicator of relative standing in a value hierarchy. Thus, an increase in the number of laymen per clergyman in the same society over time could be interpreted as reflecting a decline in the value standing of the religious tradition for which that clergy is a carrier.

This ratio is, of course, only one aspect of historical role analysis which will be brought to bear upon a systematic description and interpretation of the interplay between state church pastors, parish school teachers, lay preachers, pupils, and parents between about 1740 and 1891. Most of our attention will be upon the religious consequences of educational role system continuities, contradictions, and changes with particular reference to belief system and organizational diversification. The process of secularization will constitute a minor though recurrent theme in chapters 2 through 5 and then will be brought into focus as a major summarizing device in the final chapter.

Chapter 2 encompasses the one-hundred-year time-span up to about 1840 during which the role system in Norway within which elemental reading skills were transmitted to the rural laity remained almost unchanged. Parish school teachers were part of the infrastructure of the religious order. They served as ancillary personnel facilitating, above all, one role task of the clergy: preparation of children for Confirmation. Essentially the same textbook was used for that purpose throughout the entire period. While it is axiomatic that a "constant" cannot explain a variable, my major objective will be to show how cumulative contradictions within this system contributed both to a fundamental cleavage in popular definitions of religiosity and the incipient laicization of spiritual initiative.

Economically, the close of this period (*c.* 1840) predates Norway's industrial take-off point by about sixty years.[16] Moreover, the shift from a subsistence to a money economy began to accelerate in rural areas, most notably after 1850. Thus, while regional variations in economic organization, productivity, and growth during the preceding century were not static and provided differential preconditions for both common school development and potential religious innovation, their persuasive power as explanatory variables requires at least some qualification.

Political sources of change would seem more immediate and demonstrable. Given an established territorial church with a monopoly control of parish-level educational development wherein the clergy constituted an integral part of the official ruling strata (*embettsstand*), such an assertion is more than plausible. The most dramatic change in the context of this religio-educational system occurred when Norway regained significant control over her internal affairs with the forced transfer of ultimate political authority from Denmark to Sweden in 1814[17] as a part of a Great Power European settlement at the close of the Napoleonic Wars. This included a shift in the locus of many religious and educational policy decisions from an absolutist setting in Copenhagen to Oslo, where a potential for more popular initiative in these affairs derived from the Constitution of that year. These possibilities were realized most significantly during the 1840s when a series of political and religious "events" altered the conditions of clergy/laity relationships in several consequential ways which became more visible historically after 1850.

Chapters 3, 4, and 5 encompass a period in Norwegian societal development (1840–1891) during which traditional life expectations were being disrupted at an unprecedented level. The population, which had grown from 723,618 to 1,328,471 between 1769 and 1845 (85%), increased to 2,000,917 (93%) between 1845 and 1891. Internal migration, while only partly revealed by the relative growth of urban populations, accelerated rapidly after 1845. The percentage of urban residents in the population, which had grown by only 3.3% (8.9 to 12.2%) between 1769 and 1845, had increased another 11% (12.2 to 23.7%) by 1891. Concurrently, Norway, which ranked second only to Ireland as a nation of emigrants during the nineteenth century, experienced the departure of some 418,000 persons between 1845 and 1891, in contrast to only 6,200 during the previous decade, 1836–1845. These demographic trends both reflected and conditioned underlying transformations in the Norwegian political economy. The economy, while still largely preindustrial, had been undergoing a rapid though regionally variable monetization of its exchange system as the primary sector (forestry, fishing, agriculture, mining) was increasingly rationalized and oriented toward domestic and foreign markets. Politically, the *embettsstand* (official strata), which included the clergy, lost their centuries-old control over the state apparatus after a sustained period (*c.* 1869 to 1884) of partisan mobilization and conflict with an ascendant bourgeois Left. This issued in their subordination to a parliamentary majority after 1884.[18] We will return to these controversies in chapter 6.

Chapter 3 contains an effort to delimit the magnitude and regional distribution of organized lay activism within Norway's total population. This preliminary attempt to construct a broadly representative picture of popular religiosity is based, primarily, upon a quantitative, longitudinal analysis of lay mobilization within The Norwegian Inner-Mission Society between 1868 and 1894. Two other organized forms of religious expression for which some quantitative evidence is available – dissenter groups and foreign mission societies – are examined in order to refine the range of diversity as well as to estimate more fully the actual magnitude of popular religious activism.

Chapter 4 is focused upon elite educational experience and styles of religious (and nonreligious) expression, particularly as related to the processes of professional labor-force differentiation and the democratization of clerical social origins. The secularizing significance of these developments is expanded upon in chapter 6.

Chapter 5 resumes (from chapter 2) our analysis of that formal system within which reading skills and religious knowledge were being transmitted to the middle and lower strata of the rural laity. The social organization and content of modern Norway's elementary educational experience was in many respects initiated during this period, above all after the school law of 1860. By 1891, fixed school locations as required by that legislation had almost totally displaced the old ambulatory system described in chapter 2. Concurrently, the educational labor force began to break away from its position as part of the infrastructure of the religious order and become an increasingly autonomous educational force. Alternative worlds of meaning and new life opportunities became accessible to lower social strata on a massive basis for the first time, if only on the printed page. Combining these emergent symbolic resources with the accelerated disruption of traditional life expectations, some measure of ideological diversity both "religious" and "secular" was inevitable.

Direct, broadly representative empirical indicators of such ideological changes are simply nonexistent except insofar as historical records of voting behavior can be viewed as such. In chapters 4 and 5 I have constructed an alternative approach to this problem by comparing, where possible, diocesan and provincial variations in selected characteristics of the educational and religious labor force between about 1860 and 1891, including some less reliable and representative data on lay preachers. The several tables devoted to this description are interpreted in the context of their respective histories as these relate to each other and our central concern with exploring the interplay between mass educational development and popular religious change.

Finally, chapter 6 summarizes and supplements the discussion thus far. First, an overview of the more central explanatory sketches regarding educational systemic sources of religious diversification is provided. Secondly, some of the several ambiguities of secularization in Norway before 1891 are explored, using Glock and Stark's five dimensions of religiosity as an organizing device. This entails drawing together several observations made earlier as well as exploring some regional variations in patterns of political mobilization regarded as indirect indicators of secularity.

2. Clerical generations, educational role systems, and lay religiosity, 1740–1840

The conversion of Norway from paganism to Medieval Roman Catholicism (*c.* 1030) and the transition five hundred years later to Reformation Lutheranism obviously entailed programs of re-education without recourse to programs of mass literacy production as a means to these changing ends.[1] Even after the Reformation (1536), the major modes of religous expression among the laity were participation in life-cycle and annual ritual occasions and the rote memorization of doctrinal statements. We may imagine, however, that as the Lutheran sermon and congregational hymn singing displaced the Catholic sacramental emphasis in Sunday services, the intellectual and ideological dimensions of popular religiosity were thereby somewhat expanded and deepened.[2]

A crucial break in this system occurred with the first sustained effort to promote mass literacy as a concomitant to the reintroduction of Confirmation as a life-cycle ritual occasion under Pietist auspices in 1736. The very partial ascendency of this clerical party over their Orthodox predecessors and opponents in state church administration and at the University of Copenhagen, where all pastors were trained for the parishes of Denmark–Norway, was facilitated by the Pietist proclivities of Christian VI. Later in the century, Rationalists began to displace Pietists at these centers of power and training, aided in their turn by the religious preference and/or indifference of elite figures within the administrative structure of Danish absolutism. Thus, a third distinguishable theological orientation appeared at the clerical level in the religous order.[3]

These variants of a single official doctrinal system were neither internally homogeneous nor mutually exclusive. Clerical and Herrnhut Pietists came in conflict with each other and responded differently to conservative, moderate, and radical varieties of (Wolfian) rationalism. All these factions shared a concern for the advancement of literacy, the Pietists with a particular view to religious awakening and the Rationalists intent upon popular enlightenment of a more instrumental character.[4]

The relative dominance of these three perspectives during the eighteenth and early nineteenth centuries has usually been expressed in terms based on certain assumptions about the training experience of clerical generations. Given life tenure for all parish clergy, if we assume that the parish-level conduct of a given theological student cohort was shaped by his training, we may infer that by about 1780, representatives of all three positions coexisted in the Norwegian church. Working on these assumptions (with qualifications), Dagfinn Mannsaaker has been able to demonstrate in comprehensive quantitative terms that Rationalists reached their highest point of dominance about 1815. They began to be displaced thereafter by a fourth clerical generation trained at the newly established (1811) University of Oslo. Twenty years later, these students of Professors Hersleb and Stenersen served all but about 25 percent of the Norwegian parishes. By 1845, the transition from Copenhagen rationalism to an Oslo blend containing elements of the previous three with significant Grundtvigian strains was complete.[5]

The relative impact of these four clerical definitions of religiosity upon corresponding generations of the laity has been a matter of plausible conjecture and some scattered empirical evidence.[6] Very briefly, the overall pattern until at least 1800 appears to have been one of passive orthodoxy for something over 95 percent of the population. The basis for this assertion is simply the absence of any broadly representative direct evidence to the contrary.[7]

The evidence for Pietist influence is most tangible. Some clerical Pietists were distinguished by efforts to mobilize their parishioners into voluntary organizations composed of awakened Christians engaged in a variety of devotional practices. Orthodox clerics attached these *ecclesiola in ecclesia* (churches within the church) as potential hotbeds of doctrinal error and organizational separatism. Clerical Rationalists, on the other hand, while sharing some of these separatist apprehensions, regarded such lay enthusiasm (*svermeri*) as an irrational block to their programs of popular enlightenment. Separatist concerns were less justified in Norway than in Denmark. Those varieties of Norwegian Pietism which managed to sustain their quiet existence over more extended time periods remained small in number, almost exclusively urban in distribution, and, finally, to a greater extent than in Denmark, under effective clerical control.[8]

Educational role systems and lay religiosity

The shift from congregational catechizing under Orthodox clergymen to the more individualized preparation of children for Confirmation at the age of fourteen could hardly have been inconsequential for later styles of religious expression. Given the further fact that this instruction was conducted not in the parish church or by ordained clerics, but in farm homes by ambulatory lay teachers under necessarily limited clerical surveillance, we may surmise that the preconditions for more autonomous styles of lay religiosity were significantly enhanced and their historical visibility, as it were, increased.

Common school teachers of two distinct types coexisted in the Norwegian parishes by 1840. First in order of appearance were those parish deacons (*degn*) whose positions were an integral part of church life before Pietist clerics initiated their new educational program. After 1740 these men were gradually outnumbered by ambulatory school teachers (*omgangsskolelaerer*), who constituted an overwhelming majority of the educational labor force until after 1860.[9]

The more commonly used role labels in Norwegian for deacons were *klokker* (sexton, bell ringer) or *kirkesanger* (one who leads congregational hymn singing), which describe some of their more prominent church duties. These unordained clerical assistants stood at the bottom of the church hierarchy. Unlike the parish minister (*sogneprest*), they were usually recruited from and supported by the locality in which they worked. The rural clergy, while in closer and more frequent interaction with their laities than other royal officials, remained outsiders by virtue of their training, language, social and geographic origins, status distance within the parish, and a pattern of career mobility which meant that they seldom served out their professional lives in the same locality.

Each parish, depending on the population size and distribution within it, contained one or more churches for which a single pastor was responsible. Larger urban and some rural parishes might provide this man with a curate (*kapellan*), who served in such a position until appointed to his own post. Given the discrepancy between the number of regular clergy and the locations for which they were responsible, services could not be held every Sunday.

There is some evidence that a deacon was permitted or encouraged to conduct a modified service on those Sundays when his pastor served elsewhere. These *messefallsgudstjenester* (services without sacrament or preaching), or *klokkarmessor*, usually consisted of reading the liturgically prescribed text for that Sunday and a sermon selected by the pastor, as well as congregational hymn singing and catechization.[10] This practice appears to have been most common in those parishes where church locations were most widely scattered, as along the Swedish border in eastern Norway. It may be suggested that insofar as this actually occurred, deacons provided a non-professional role model for more autonomous religious action by the laity. The dangers inherent in this practice were recognized by some church officials, and it was limited accordingly in its use.

The new school ordinance expanded the deacon's educational role tasks to include preparation for Confirmation, a more intensive, focused activity than congregational catechizing had been. Those few school buildings (*fasteskoler*) which were constructed near some main parish churches (*hovedkirker*) before 1837 were served by these deacons. Most of them, however, were among the first ambulatory teachers in their parishes. It is probable that these men were usually more qualified both religiously and educationally than those non-deacon teachers who later constituted a majority of the educational labor force as the system expanded. Their traditionally established position, more frequent interaction with the clergy, higher economic support derived from non-educational but religious duties, suggest this.

Moving now to those teachers who were not also deacons, let us begin with a tangible failure. The well-intentioned school ordinance of 1739, as Hermon Rugge expressed it, had but one fault. It was never brought to life through central financial support and implementation.[11] Instead, the program was turned over to diocesan and parish authorities to fight out with their laities. Out of this continuing conflict between the economic interests of the peasantry and the educational aspirations of the clergy came the ambulatory school teacher.

These men were seasonal workers who assumed this role temporarily as a supplement to their regular livelihoods until more lucrative and prestigious opportunities opened up in the rural economy. Payment for services consisted almost, but not entirely, of food and lodging provided at those farm homes scattered throughout the parish where children were assembled for instruction during a few weeks of the winter months. Exemption from military service of seven years' duration constituted a further inducement, which may have been decisive in many cases. Turnover rates were high. Length of active school service may have been influenced by the alternative of military conscription as well as more general economic conditions.

It seems plausible to assert that if one learns more by teaching than being taught, then these ex-school teachers were among the most literate segment of the rural population's middle and lower strata. If the deacon/teacher combination produced, on the average, even more literate men, the reason, in addition to those cited above, may be found in the probability that turnover rates were lower, given their additional income and the greater likelihood that such teaching became a life-long career.

During its first century of development, the expansion of this system through an increase in the number of teachers per clergyman was largely dependent upon the allocation of local parish resources. Some external support became available when Rationalists gained control of the central church administration in Copenhagen and diverted funds intended for

Table 2.1. *National aggregate ratios of clergy and teachers to total population and each other, 1815–1845*

Year	Laity/Clergy	Laity/Teachers	Teachers/Clergy	Total population
1815	2,214	492	4.5	885,431
1825	2,978	618	4.8	1,051,318
1835	2,632	577	4.6	1,194,827
1845	2,955	564	5.2	1,328,471

Sources: Laity/Clergy ratios are from D. Mannsaaker, *Det Norske Presteskapet* (Oslo, 1954), p. 72, table 7. All others are computed from Vilhelm Aubert *et al.*, *The Professions in Norwegian Social Structure 1720–1955* (Oslo,1961), vol. I, table 1.

additional clergymen to parish school needs. This practice was symptomatic of a broader policy with fundamental implications for the clergy's control over the growing number of parish teachers, as well as their more general impact on the laity.[12]

Some quantitative evidence is available which will enable us to examine these changing relationships between clergy, teachers, and general population more graphically. Table 2.1 presents three ratios at ten-year intervals from 1815 to 1845 which indicate the number of laymen per clergyman and common school teacher as well as fluctuations in the number of teachers for every clergyman at a national aggregate level. Comparable data bearing on these relationships before 1815 are available only for the laity/clergy ratio, which increased from 1,300 in 1750 to 1,884 in 1800.

Several relational changes can be inferred from these ratios. First, as the laity/clergy ratio more than doubled (1750–1845), direct clerical influence on the laity declined. Secondly, the educational dimension of this communication gap was reduced via those deacons and ambulatory teachers whose numbers expanded more rapidly than did those of their clerical superiors. Finally, given the more intensive and extensive interaction between teachers and, at a minimum, the school-age population of each parish, an increase in the teacher/clergy ratio enhanced the potential for a kind of "teacher/laity religiosity" in tension with clerical expectations.[13]

Let us look more closely at some of the formal attributes of this ambulatory system. Teachers met pupils in farm homes, with some host adults present during instruction. Locations were selected with a view to maximizing accessibility to the largest number of children and thereby facilitating regular attendance.

Each parish was divided into school districts (*omgangsskolekretzer*) composed of several teaching locations (*roder*), i.e., farmhouses. According to Dokka, by 1837, "the average number of districts per parish was 5.75 and, within these, the average number of *roder*, 3.80." These figures also indicate the number of teachers – one per district – as well as the average number of settings in which they met their assembled pupils. "The number of days a teacher held school at the different locations varied strongly; it was dependent, in the first place, upon the farm's size and the economic circumstances of the owner. At one farm, school might last one day and at another, ten. Some places where dwellings were particularly scattered, additional locations were established within the single *roder*."[14]

The exposure of children to this system varied within and between parishes, primarily according to the economic life-situation of their parents and regional variations in economic support. The range of variations in frequency of pupil–teacher interaction was probably wider in the eastern dioceses (Oslo, Trondhjem), where status differentials within the population were both greater in number and more rigidly defined than in the western and southern dioceses of Bergen and Agder.[15] On the other hand, it is probable that the average frequency of educational contacts was higher in the east than the south and west, where the economic base for educational support was lower.[16]

The average number of school days available to children in rural areas according to the first (1837) comprehensive statistical report from all parishes to the Ministry of Church and Education was 47.5 days, or about seven weeks. Actual frequency of attendance was significantly lower than this. A second series of parish reports issued in 1853 contained some less comprehensive evidence bearing on this source of variation. Average attendance for those districts reporting was 30.5 days. It would seem highly probable, as Dokka observes, that attendance levels were even lower for those districts not reporting or whose returns on this item proved unusable. Finally, a widespread opinion among contemporary observers of the ambulatory school scene was that these figures were somewhat inflated and that actual attendance was still lower.[17]

All these averages, of course, obscure marked variations within and between dioceses and parishes. As we have seen, the number of days an ambulatory teacher might instruct at a given farm home could range from about one to ten, depending on the relative affluence of the several hosts. The extent to which children could or would avail themselves of these differentially distributed opportunities varied directly with the economic life-situation of their parents. Thus, in the more stratified dioceses of eastern Norway, the children of agricultural laborers and tenant farmers missed these opportunities more frequently than those of small or large farm owners whose labor power was less crucial to family well being.

Pontoppidan religiosity and the clergy

The gradual expansion and actual effectiveness before 1827 of this system whereby rural parishioners were to reach some consequential level of literacy is a matter for plausible conjecture, since comprehensive statistical reports are not available. All evidence indicates that the formal relationships between preachers, teachers, pupils, and their parents remained essentially unchanged. What did change were the theological orientations of the clergy in control of the system. *A priori*, the impact of these clerical styles upon lay religiosity should have been greatly enhanced via their parish school teachers. The teachers were selected from and trained within a self-perpetuating system. Superior performance at Confirmation comprised the fundamental qualification for their teaching position. Once initiated, they simply reproduced themselves under clerical guidance.

The single most stable and universally shared feature of this educational experience was its core curriculum. Bishop Erik Pontoppidan's *Explanation of Luther's Little Catechism* (*Sannhet til Gudfryktighet*) was authorized in 1738 and remained, in gradually abbreviated versions, the exclusive textbook for common school instruction in the Norwegian parishes long after its use was discontinued in Denmark.[18] All children, beginning at the age of seven, were expected to memorize this text through catechistic exchange with their teachers so as to be able to answer their pastor, dean, or bishop's questions on Confirmation day, normally at the age of fourteen.

Rote learning of a single text cannot be equated with functional literacy, if by that we mean the acquisition of generalized reading skills transferable to other printed matter of comparable difficulty. Qualified observers of the educational scene around 1850 estimated that such "rote literacy" best described the reading skills of, perhaps, half Norway's population.[19] Nevertheless, literacy, whether rote or functional, is not illiteracy, and a closer examination of its content (Pontoppidan) and the process whereby it was inculcated is fundamental to any assessment of lay religiosity after 1740.

Erik Pontoppidan's (1698–1764) most significant long-term influence as Pietist theologian and churchman was indirect. His successive positions as palace pastor (*hofprest*), theological professor, Bishop of Bergen diocese, and university official (*prokansler*) were all elite posts. At this level, whatever impact his policies may have had were often either weakened by Orthodox counter-elite resistance to implementation or partly cancelled as theological Rationalists gained control. The crucial exception came with the establishment of Confirmation (1736) through which Pontoppidan's *Explanation* was gradually institutionalized over the next one hundred and fifty years within the religious life cycle of Norway's total population. Except for a series of abbreviations, its fundamental Pietistic character remained unchanged despite partial incongruence with later styles of clerical religiosity. Perhaps the most persuasive indicator of its quasi-canonical status can be derived from the bitter, widespread, and effective resistance of the Norwegian laity when an attempt was made to introduce a significantly revised edition in the 1840s.[20]

Pontoppidan's impact upon styles of religiosity must have varied according to the life-situation and experience of the recipient. Most simply, the encounter with his text was necessarily different for a university-trained minister from that of his teachers and parishioners. Let us consider some of these variations and their sources more systematically.

Pietist theologians never gained the sustained, dominant position within the Copenhagen faculty held by their Orthodox and, later, Rationalist opponents. According to Oluf Kolsrud, only a small minority of clerical candidates aligned themselves with the Pietist church party as a result of formal training during their student years.[21] On the other hand, once assigned to a parish, their practical pastoral duties included a very heavy commitment of time and energy to religious education. Given the universal, obligatory use of Pontoppidan for this purpose and the many years of confirming children and selecting parish teachers according to its criteria, we may reasonably conclude that such a recurrent experience constituted the single most pervasive source of Pietist influence upon the Norwegian clergy. Their attitudes toward Pontoppidan's relatively high-church, Halle variety of pietism probably varied according to their training, theological orientation, and, above all, their views on the nature of the church and the clerical office within it. Men of Orthodox or Rationalist persuasions presumably regarded their parishes as official units of the territorial church system and all baptized parishioners therein as more or less equal members, spiritually subordinate to the clerical office. Orthodox criteria of religiosity stressed ritual participation and formal commitment to official doctrine. Rationalists emphasized the moral/ethical implications of the Christian message for daily conduct in their more consequential definition of religiosity.

Pontoppidan's *Explanation* systematically inculcated a contrary view on several of these points. First and foremost, without a transforming awareness of the Living Christ and Him Crucified, all doctrinal orthodoxy, ritual conformity, and good works are a snare and a delusion leading the complacent on to eternal damnation. All these may be necessary as facilitating conditions for or evidence of that living faith – but they are fatal substitutes.[22]

The implications of this message for popular conceptions of religiosity are at least partly self-evident. The assessment of the extent to which this experiential definition of their spiritual standing was actually accepted by the laity is obviously more problematic. If we rely on historically visible evidence for the period between 1750 and 1850 its impact would seem very limited, differentially distributed by region, and somewhat variable in its actual content.

Part of the variance in this impact over time and by parish or region may have been due to clerical turnover and distribution. Thus, as we have seen, organizational evidence for Pietist influence surfaced primarily in those parishes and areas served by and accessible to pastors of this persuasion. Even within this relatively small and transitory church party, significant factions appeared in tension with Pontoppidan's *clerically* centered variety of Halle pietism. Thus, many of the most influential Norwegian pastoral Pietists had aligned themselves with the more radical Herrnhut faction during their student days in Copenhagen. Insofar as they disagreed with some of Pontoppidan's formulations they may have introduced a sense of exegetical variety into their parishes and thereby provided even further ground for religious differences.

The Orthodox apparently recognized that these ideas were not likely to bolster clerical authority or religious unity within their parishes. Their universalistic doctrine of the church as composed of all obedient, baptized communicants stood in tension with these particularistic, experiential criteria for membership in God's True Congregation. Just how this tension may have influenced their behavior while selecting and supervising the activities of parish teachers who actually did the immediate work of preparing children for Confirmation day is, to my knowledge, simply unknown.

Let us consider some of the more plausible possibilities. First of all, the experienced level of doctrinal dissonance was not necessarily very high, since Pontoppidan's *Explanation* was certainly no handbook for heretics. His orthodoxy, in a generic sense, was not directly open to question. Luther's *Little Catechism* was, after all, the foundation upon which his *Explanation* was constructed. Pontoppidan's first, unabbreviated edition contained 759 questions, answers, and appropriate Biblical citations.[23] These dealt systematically with each petition of the Lord's Prayer, the Ten Commandments, each element of the Creed, the sacraments of Baptism and Communion, etc. Pontoppidan himself indicated a rather large number of questions which did not need to be included among those for literal memorization by the children.

Even so, its length proved unworkable, and later editions were abridged still further. Now while the entire text was supposed to be memorized, there was room for relative emphasis both during the training sessions with teachers and most certainly on Confirmation day itself, since only a small fraction of these questions could be asked during the time available. In short, both Orthodox and Rationalist parish ministers could systematically neglect those elements most incongruent with their own views.

If and when some contradictions could not be glossed over, at least two possibilities were open: reinterpretation and/or compartmentalization. There is some anecdotal evidence which suggests that Pontoppidan's religiosity was regarded as being appropriate for the middle and lower strata among the laity composed of small land-owners, tenant farmers, and agricultural laborers. We will have occasion to examine this possibility later when considering lay encounters with the text. Here it suffices to say that Pontoppidan's formulations could not restrict clerical presentations in other contexts. For all pastoral generations the central, recurrent religious encounter with their laities was in the Sunday services, restricted only by an officially prescribed annual cycle of Biblical texts which were supposed to serve as the take-off point for the sermon. Here, depending on his orientation, the pastor could reinforce, qualify, ignore, and/or contradict Pontoppidan, at least by implication. That this actually occurred in forms noticeable to the laity is one of the most recurrent generalizations made by some historians of the Hauge Movement. According to neo-orthodox church historians of the late nineteenth century, Hauge's major opponents and persecutors were Rationalist pastors who devoted their sermons to new farming practices and other worldly concerns.[24] This caricature has since been strongly qualified, but the fundamental picture of sermons devoted to moral–ethical matters, often of a practical character, has, to my knowledge, remained.

Finally, since clerical orientations were neither mutually exclusive nor internally homogeneous, it is possible that a dialectic interchange within and between these camps issued in a partial blending of emphases. Professors Hersleb and Stenersen, trained at Copenhagen during the height of Rationalist power, usually are described as representing such a blend with some additional elements added through their friendship with Grundtvig.[25] As we have seen, their students gradually displaced Copenhagen Rationalists and thereby introduced a fourth theological variant into the Norwegian parishes.

Given this possibility of a dialectic and the use of Pontoppidan, which provided both continuity and a common textual base for the clergy's encounters with the laity at Confirmation, it seems likely that the experiential demand and the Pietist vocabulary for expressing religious sensibility could not be ignored and became part of their self-awareness, if only as a negative reference point.

Teachers, Haugean activists, and laicization

The social origins and life experience of deacons and teachers contrasted sharply with the Copenhagen–Oslo trained clerical outsiders whose language and life styles limited intimate communication with their parishioners. Any attempt to assess the independent significance of Norway's common school system as one factor contributing to religious continuity and change must deal in plausible reconstructions of the teachers' intellectual world. Their encounter with Pontoppidan was, of course, more sustained and intense than was that of the average laymen. It constituted their only shared experience with something like systematic theology.

Evidence regarding the availability of other printed materials is more problematic, with the important exception of hymnbooks for congregational singing. Here again, as in the case of Pontoppidan, their use was part of an established pattern. On the other hand, unlike the Confirmation text, officially promoted alternatives became available though not widely accepted by the laity. Kingo's Orthodox hymnal, authorized in 1699, retained its official monopoly until the 1770s, when an unsuccessful attempt was made to replace it with Ove Guldberg's collection which tried to combine the three major competing theological perspectives within the church. This proved to be too conservative for the enlightened elite and too contrived and complex for the ordinary layman. A third alternative, the *Evangelical Christian Hymnbook*, authorized in 1798 and composed almost entirely of "Rationalist verse," proved even less acceptable. The widespread and intense hostility evoked by this collection among the laity (and conservative clergy) provides some indirect evidence for the efficacy of earlier indoctrination via Kingo and Pontoppidan. The doctrinal innovations contained therein were simply too glaring to be ignored by those who had at least memorized those quasi-canonical texts.[26]

The distribution of Bibles and popular devotional literature was dependent largely upon the voluntary decisions of individuals to allocate a portion of their meager resources to such acquisitions. Diffusion of these and other reading materials appears to have varied according to social strata and region, and to have accelerated most rapidly around 1800.[27]

Teachers were likely to have earlier and more sustained access to this wider religious world in print than did the average rural layman. Given their closer and more frequent interaction with the clergy, whose book collections, more often than not, were the only ones available in rural parishes, this assumption of relative accessibility seems plausible.

Max Weber, in discussing the impact of proletarian intellectuals upon religious developments, includes "elementary school teachers of all sorts" among their number without really elaborating upon the context or character of their activities or influence.[28] Our Norwegian teachers may indeed have constituted a kind of lower strata "literati" who were likely to contain a disproportionate number of incipient, nonclerical exegetes. Given the exigencies of their pedagogic experience, some explanation by the teachers of Pontoppidan's *Explanation* to their pupils must have been inevitable. At an absolute minimum, given the fact that Pontoppidan's Danish was often radically different from the Norwegian dialects of both teachers and pupils, philological explications must have become an integral part of the teaching process, if the educational outcome was to be more than the repetition of almost meaningless phrases.[29] If we assume that solutions to these linguistic problems were gradually routinized in consultation with the Copenhagen-trained clergy, the possibilities for interpretive variations still remain, particularly as non-Pietist clerical superiors may have suggested them in sermon or conversation.

If teaching encouraged ambulatory exegetes in Confirmation classes, it did not produce any significant number of autonomous lay activists comparable to Hans Nielsen Hauge and his co-workers. An examination of this movement's development will reveal more about the scope and content of popular literacy as well as about the incipient laicization of religious life than any other single historically visible phenomena.

As the first generation of pastors trained in and appointed from Oslo moved into the parishes, some of them encountered representatives of an already established lay movement which had become national in scope despite twenty years of rather uneven efforts by clerical and civil authorities to repress it. This movement was initiated (1796) and led by Hans Nielsen Hauge (1771–1824), and was loosely coordinated, even before his death, by local lay elders whom he had designated or indirectly approved.[30] Hauge and his friends denounced false teachers among the clergy but not the clerical office as such, with its ritual system prerogatives. The teaching and preaching role tasks were another matter. Here they initiated a pattern of lay preaching which continued to develop in diverse forms throughout the nineteenth century.

Sociologically, this role system innovation was of vastly greater significance for subsequent religious differentiation than any doctrinal deviations contained in Hauge's numerous and widely distributed writings. The Norwegian clergy, whatever their partisan differences, could agree that public preaching was their exclusive prerogative as defined by Article Fourteen of the Augsburg Confession. Religious gatherings not restricted to the immediate family circle (except those under clerical surveillance) remained in violation of the Conventicle Act of 1741 until its revocation in 1842.

Haugean organizational patterns were much more diffuse, being based on an exchange of circular letters and visits between more or less influential elders and friends. The Haugean precedent provided an heroic historical model for lay preachers rather than a sustained, coherent institutional challenge to clerical authority.

Hauge's travels, between 1796 and 1804, encompassed a variable number of parishes in every Norwegian province south of Finnmark. Unlike the travel accounts of elite observers,[31] his were based upon rather intimate participation in the daily life of those farm families with whom he stayed. Scattered passages in his autobiographical works contain descriptions of life styles in different regions, including dress, diet, entertainment, degrees of receptivity to religious conversation, levels of education, and, finally, how well his books sold or were selling.

The magnitude of Hauge's book market indicates a good deal about the educational achievements of the common school system. For example, he reports that two editions of his *Christian Doctrine* were published in Copenhagen during 1800–1801 and "shipped to the various towns in accordance with the instructions I had left with the printer. Forty-five hundred copies of this book were printed in the first edition and five thousand in the second edition."[32] More generally, it has been estimated that "of the eight most important works he produced between 1796 and 1800, 50,000 to 60,000 copies were printed and distributed and were read by at least 100,000 persons."[33] If we consider that the total population at this time was about 883,000, it becomes dramatically obvious that functional literacy, while probably still unevenly distributed, was not the monopoly of any single stratum or group.

Systematic research on the social composition of Hauge's friends and opponents provides a major source of evidence on the scope and content of religious differentiation within Norway's population at this period. His final arrest and imprisonment in 1804 were followed by a comprehensive official investigation of Haugean activities, including voluminous reports from all levels of church and state administration. Of the one hundred and fifty parish ministers who responded to a question about remedial action, twenty-two indicated they could handle the problem themselves, and only three expressed unqualified approval of his activities.[34]

Given this almost unanimous negative reaction, it seems reasonable to infer that, regardless of theological orientation, many of their subordinate educational co-workers responded in a somewhat similar fashion. Mannsaaker constructs a persuasive argument for the view that a majority of parish bailiffs (*lensmenn*), whose status at the bottom of the civil hierarchy was similar to that of deacons in the church's rank order, shared the hostility expressed by their civil and religious superiors. Hauge's description of his encounters with all levels of officialdom, from bishops and provincial governors to parish pastors and those bailiffs who arrested him recurrently, while not as uniformly negative, suggests at best a picture of tolerance at the top and occasional sympathy at the bottom.

He makes explicit reference to direct encounters with only one teacher and one deacon (*klokker*). The first assaulted him physically, and the second attacked him in public for undermining the educational work of a lifetime. These must be seen as dramatic episodes rather than representative cases of his probable encounters with teachers. On the other hand, his published condemnation of false teachers, presumably directed toward the clergy, could have included these educators and been experienced by them as directed toward themselves as well.

The distinction between "educated" (*opdragelses*) and "awakened" (*vaekkelses*) Christianity, which became and remained central symbols in the rhetoric of religious controversy after 1850, was at least partly generated by contradictions within the system of religious education. Pontoppidan's experiential religiosity was first activated on a national scale by the Haugeans, for whom passive Confirmation was not enough. Pastors and teachers, on the other hand, were obliged to be universalistic in their preparation of children for and conduct of this ritual occasion. It seems probable that some teachers and their pupils were awakened during this process without becoming activists in the Haugean sense. If so, they remain even less visible historically than some of Hauge's quieter Friends. There is, of course, the possibility that ex-school teachers were among his following without being so identified, since the title had only transitory value as a term of social reference.

The focus in this book upon preachers and teachers as prime agents of religious continuity, coherence, and unintended differentiation has necessarily neglected informal religious socialization within the family. The historiographic reasons for this neglect are obvious. School and church activities are a matter of public routine and partial record. Family religious practices are not. In 1834, school authorities recommended that "when the family in the house where school is being held is gathered in the evening, the school teacher, if so desired, particularly during the long winter evenings, ought to read from one or another useful book, according to the pastor's recommendation, as well as holding an evening devotional by reading an evening prayer and singing a hymn with the people of the house."[35] This recommendation probably described a practice of frequent but not universal occurrence for several decades before it was made official. If so, it served as a variant on those book-centered home devotionals conducted by some family heads which became possible when and where adequate reading skills were developed.

Here was a custom and a related book market which Hauge knew from his own childhood and which provided him with an opening for those edifying conversations which, "if so desired," turned into more or less public assemblies of unrelated persons in violation of the Conventicle Act. It is tempting to see in the 1834 recommendation a belated attempt to compete with lay activists by mobilizing parish teachers to meet some of those needs both revealed and generated by them.

Some further implications of this plausible systemic tension between Haugeans and the educational labor force for religious differentiation within rural Norway can now be considered in light of what is known or can be inferred about their respective social origins and relationships.

First, as we have seen, ambulatory teaching was a part-time, temporary career. Given the low prestige and remuneration experienced by men engaged in this activity, it is not surprising to find that they usually came from the homes of tenant farmers and small land-holders.[36] The experienced social distance between strata was much greater in eastern than in western and southern Norway, where small holdings predominated and social interaction between owners, tenants, and farm laborers, in and out of work situations, was closer.[37] Given this regional contrast, the impact of Pontoppidan transmitted primarily by this lower-stratum "intelligentsia" might have varied by region and stratum: that is, styles of religiosity attributable to Pontoppidan might have been more evenly distributed in western than eastern Norway. If so, we may hypothesize that this western region's historical reputation for higher levels of piety and lay activism is partially traceable to this source: i.e., greater status intimacy between pupils, teachers, and parents in tension with a socially distant clergy.

The class interests and life styles of large land-holders in eastern Norway stood in sharper contrast with their workers, tenants, and small land-holding neighbors. Ambulatory teachers could almost be defined as part-time household servants who used their larger homes as occasional classrooms for the instruction of a socially mixed group of pupils. Given the variations by strata in availability and utilization of these educational opportunities, we might expect that the children of large land owners were more likely to become functionally literate. Even if the children from lower strata attained some measure of functional or rote literacy, however, such skills were likely to die through disuse after Confirmation.

Insofar as these status cleavages impinged upon the educational process, we may hypothesize that some variant of Pontoppidan's experiential demands were most likely to be accepted and sustained by children from middle and lower strata in view of the greater status proximity between such pupils and their teachers. If we extend this principle of status proximity and teacher influence to larger land-holders and their children, then the encounter with Pontoppidan should have issued in a different modal style of religious expression, characterized, perhaps, by formal ritual participation, orthodox ideological commitment, and a more differentiated range of religious and other knowledge derived from reading. Finally, we may surmise that status pride would inhibit participation in modes of religious expression identified with their social inferiors.

Haugeanism, as the most widespread variant on Pontoppidan religiosity, required an egalitarian fellowship of all believers in principled tension with traditional status cleavages. An examination of what is known about its social composition provides a partial empirical check on these familiar generalizations relating life situations to styles of religiosity.[38]

First, given the relationship between status and historical visibility, it is not surprising that we know more about Hauge's opponents than his friends. Their reports to the central government provide a major, systematic, if biased source of information about the magnitude, distribution, and social composition of those variable fractions of the laity identified with or in opposition to the movement. Here again, historiographic availability is greatest for Hauge's more active co-workers whose legal encounters left official records as well as an honored place in Haugean accounts of their efforts. Historical sociologists and others have usually had to assume that, in the absence of representative data on its less active following, an examination of a movement's leadership provides the single most reliable and valid indicator of its social composition. This must serve as an assumption in the present case as well.

Whatever other variations there may have been in their initial life situations, Hauge and his earliest co-workers in preaching and book distribution were not from the homes of large land-holders. It was only later in the movement's historical development that more affluent personalities surfaced. Among these, the most prominent were, like Hauge, migrants from rural parishes who established themselves as merchants and craft entrepreneurs, particularly in Bergen, Kristiansand, Oslo, and near Drammen. Hauge was often the initiator of such moves among his friends, not only to urban but to other rural parishes, where he discovered more promising life-situations for them.

This Haugean migration, whether as merchants, craftsmen, farmers, or lay preachers, provoked hostility toward them, not only from officials and economic competitors but also from all strata of the population. Hauge was accused of polarizing parishes and disrupting traditional authority within families as well as religious and economic life.[39]

The weight of historical evidence points to the conclusion that Hauge's appeal was strongest among his status equals or below, and weakest among those above. However, exceptions to this general pattern occurred in both directions. For example, large land-holders were reported as being particularly prominent in Eiker parish near Drammen, where Haugeans had established a paper mill which also served as a major communication center for the movement. On the other hand, Hauge encountered some uniformly hostile parishes in the south, west, and northern parts of the country, where average economic conditions were on a par with or below that of small land-holders and tenant farmers in the East Country. Clearly, degree of status proximity was not a simple determinant of audience response where regional and other localized differences could inhibit the desired effect.

Clerical diagnosticians claimed that the Haugean affliction was most prevalent among the "unenlightened" members of their parishes. The reference here, apparently, was to what they regarded as a misguided devotion to Pontoppidan, the Bible, and Kingo's hymnbook. Certainly Hauge himself, in justifying his officially deviant behavior, often appealed to these authoritative texts.[40]

Loyalty to these criteria of religiosity was hardly a Haugean monopoly, since encounters with Pontoppidan were universal, whereas mobilization in this movement seldom included more than a variable minority anywhere. Hauge encountered scattered Pietist remnants in Vestfold, Lower Telemark, Listerland (Vest Agder), and his home parish during his travels before 1800. Two localized and transitory anti-Haugean splinter groups appeared during the 1820s: the *Staerketroende* (Strong Believers) in southern Rogaland and the Feigians from Luster parish, which had been an early Haugean center at the inner reaches of the Sognefjord.

These and other more sporadic cases of lay activism appeared as Haugeanism began to exhibit that familiar routinization of the spirit indicated by their less-qualified acceptance of and by the clergy as well as a pattern of upward political and economic mobility for which they became famous.[41] The Haugean model for an activist priesthood of all believers proved irreversible, at least among awakened segments of the laity.

The clerical control system in transitions, 1814–1845

Several generations of lay encounters with Pontoppidan via the parish school system issued in widespread religious literacy and heightened sensitivity to doctrinal issues, strongly tinged by experiential criteria of religiosity. Visible activism remained a minority phenomenon largely contained within the established order. The first and most militant, incipient sectarian[42] phase of Haugeanism ended with Hauge's arrest and imprisonment in 1804. By the time his court case was settled in 1814, the conditions for potential political/religious action on the part of the laity had begun to alter significantly. Above all, the establishment of a university at Oslo (1811) and the transfer of state power from Danish absolutism to the Swedish crown, as limited by the remarkably democratic constitution of 1814, shifted the center of clerical training and control, as well as of internal political initiative, to Oslo.

A fourth clerical generation, produced by Professors Hersleb and Stenersen away from the more cosmopolitan influences of Copenhagen, began to displace the dominant Rationalists. By 1835, all but 25 percent of the Norwegian clergy was composed of students of Hersleb and Stenersen. These two men, while trained at Copenhagen, were among that small minority of Norwegian theologians who "turned away from rationalism and were on their way back to orthodox Biblical Christianity and Lutheran Confessionalism."[43] Their attitude toward the Haugeans and some other lay activists, while less hostile than that of their predecessors, left no doubt that public preaching remained a clerical monopoly.

The beginning of the end of such one-sided religious initiative was signaled by the gradual political mobilization of economically qualified segments of the rural electorate. This process culminated in the Storting of 1833, when peasant representatives gained an absolute majority for the first time. Thereafter, the redistribution of political/religious power all but eliminated the parish clergy's formal–legal control over popular expressions of religiosity. The introduction of elective communal councils in 1837 provided the institutional preconditions for political mobilization and action at the parish level for those segments of the population meeting certain property requirements. The opinions of these local councils were gathered regarding alternative legislative proposals concerned with the retention or revocation of the Conventicle Act of 1741 as well as the lifting of the total ban on non-Lutheran (but Christian) dissenter activities in Norway.[44] Revocation was successful (1842) and eliminated legal constraints upon lay preaching and popular religious assemblies for members of the state church. This opened the way for organized manifestations of popular religious differentiation *within* the established order, which accelerated thereafter. The Dissenter Law of 1845 opened Norway to the evangelistic efforts of activists *outside* the church, which further facilitated the potential diversification of religious expression.[45]

The role in and reaction to some of these and other developments within Haugean circles is instructive. First, while the movement remained fundamentally intact as a loose network of like-minded friends after Hauge's death in 1824, a process of accommodation to context had begun, as indicated by their qualified cooperation with other lay activists (e.g., Moravian Pietists) and a few clergymen sympathetic on issues of mutual concern. Concurrently, the Haugean variant on Weber's "work ethic" issued in economic ascent. This trend, in combination with their experience as lay leaders and public speakers, qualified some of the Haugeans for entry into the political process as Storting representatives. Once freedom for Lutheran lay preachers was established, most (but not all) of them mobilized against the Dissenter Law, which passed over their opposition.

Once these civil constraints were removed, effective clerical control necessarily shifted from considerable reliance on legal coercion to a traditional foundation which had undergone several modifications within the clerical role system itself, from Orthodox absolutism in 1740 to a more qualified authoritarianism one hundred years later. The unilateral character of these redefinitions declined as mass literacy provided the laity with skills and symbolic resources which enabled them to articulate in more autonomous and effective ways their own varieties of Lutheranism, including perceptions of the clerical office.

Initially, the parish school system's ambulatory educational labor force provided the structural basis for a kind of localized teacher/laity religiosity in potential tension with the expectations of clerical outsiders. Later, the Hauge movement both revealed and developed a cleavage within this structure which, it may be suggested, provided some of the preconditions for an intermediate style of educated religiosity between formal clerical universalism above and the incipient sectarian style of lay activists below. The invidious distinction between awakened and merely educated Christians which permeated the polemics of religious controversy after 1850 was partially anchored in a growing tension between common school universalism and lay movement particularism. On the other hand, as we shall see in chapter 5, accelerated educational developments, particularly after 1860, included greater role autonomy for teachers *vis-à-vis* the parish clergy. This, in combination with a more differentiated secular curriculum, provided at least the beginnings of an alternative plausibility structure[46] in qualified competition with the experiential demands of both lay activists and the Johnsonian clergy.

The relative stability and isolation of Norway's rural population began to break down in regionally variable ways after 1845 as the money economy diffused and migration to America and urban centers increased at a greatly accelerated pace.[47] Such new and ever-changing life-situations have usually been associated with the disruption of traditional modes of coping with reality, which in turn issue in the construction of more meaningful symbolic responses to the world. Despite these provocative conditions, the range and content of historically visible deviations from traditional patterns of religious conduct and belief remained remarkably limited.

The next chapter contains an attempt to construct estimates of the magnitude and regional distribution of *organized* deviations from established religious routines. Chapters 4 and 5 will refine those estimates somewhat by focusing upon the relationship between levels of educational experience and styles of religious expression as differentiated along lines of social stratification. Here, by way of anticipating some future developments, two rather dramatic episodes of popular protest during the 1840s will be sketched.

First, when Marcus Thrane,[48] founder of the first socialist movement in Norwegian history, mobilized some 26,000 to 30,000 tenant farmers, small land-owners, and workers between 1848 and 1851 in protest against their increasingly miserable life-situations, a new ideological threat surfaced. This rather mild reformist movement, given the European scene, apparently terrified both the civil and religious powers. State authorities imprisoned Thrane and broke the movement, but not before some of its religiously relevant undercurrents awakened the clergy to a new danger. These men and women from Hedmark, Buskerud, Oppland, Akershus, and other East Country provinces were unlikely to become evangelical Lutheran lay preachers or even provide a very receptive audience for such. What seems to have alarmed church authorities was the dramatic evidence this "episode" provided of lower-strata alienation from the established order. Passive participation or simple indifference, combined with a kind of endemic anticlericalism, may very well have been characteristic of this East Country stratum, but such organized hostility was not. In contrast, the Haugeans, who were never very successful in most of this same area, would have been almost welcomed as a counter force to such an expression of popular secularism. On the other hand, if Thrane's followers violated the Fourth Commandment enjoining obedience to worldly superiors, as learned in their Pontoppidan school days, the extent to which they shared his rather humanistic anti-confessionalism is more problematic. Nevertheless, something like this was imputed to the movement by authorities in the Oslo diocese where it was almost totally concentrated.[49]

An earlier crisis was initiated in 1843, when an attempt was made to introduce a revised version of Pontoppidan's *Explanation* in the parish schools. By 1852, sustained, if rather scattered, popular protest to its doctrinal implications, both real and imagined, issued in the government's providing an option whereby use of the old text could continue in those parishes desiring it. That decision was, apparently, prompted by official fears of civil disorders bordering on revolution and/or massive withdrawals from the state church and formation of free congregations, made possible by the Dissenter Law of 1845.[50]

Such resistance cannot be dismissed as simply a matter of rural, rote literalism, since abbreviated but not essentially altered versions had been accepted earlier. Pontoppidan's quasi-canonical text had survived all clerical generations as a kind of Biblical and Confessional pony for the people and the unordained exegetes among them. Contemporary observers of the common school scene, as noted earlier, estimated that about 50 percent of Norway's population had made the transition from rote to functional literacy by 1850. The Catechism controversy added weight to that probability. More to the present point, however, its resolution dramatized the potential of collective action, at least when, unlike the Thrane movement, the objectives did not threaten fundamental political economic interests of dominant strata. Finally, the published disputations generated during this conflict both sharpened old and revealed new sources of religious cleavage which were gradually institutionalized after 1850 with some far-reaching implications for the content of educational development (to be explored in chapter 5).

Einar Molland has described Norwegian religious life after 1850 as containing both awakening and secularizing trends.[51] It is hardly surprising that here, as elsewhere, the historical visibility and social distribution of these phenomena were markedly different. More generally, Molland, I believe, is correct in his interpretation of these divergent symbolic responses to a changing reality as two sides of the same fundamental process, i.e., the progressive dissolution of religious unity. The centuries-old distinction between clerical and lower-strata lay religiosity began to break down as the behavioral content and the inner meaning of being a religious person gradually fused in something closer to a single definition for those segments of the population, both lay and clerical, who were mobilized in the outer- and inner-mission movements. The distinction between awakened and, at best, merely educated Christians altered the criteria of religious diversification within Norwegian society as clerical and lay activists redefined their parishioners and neighbors as spiritual somnambulists, agents of doctrinal error and/or outright disbelievers. As these criteria gained organized expression, the cleavage between Christianity and structurally differentiated styles of secular symbolism began to widen at an accelerating pace.

3. Organizational indicators of religious differentiation in Norwegian society, 1850–1891

Constructing empirical indicators of religious differentiation within total national populations is no task either for perfectionists or scholars with a low tolerance for ambiguity. Understandably, most cliometritians have sought to gratify their desires for descriptive clarity by focusing on historical phenomena (demographic, economic, political) for which reasonably reliable and broadly representative evidence exists in the archives of nation-states with rather long histories of bureaucratic record-keeping. Where religious pluralism obtained, as in Britain, Holland, and Switzerland, such diversity had a chance of being officially relevant and thereby recorded. Currie, Gilbert, and Horsley have availed themselves of that potential in their impressive quantitative studies of church growth in Britain since 1700.[1] In Norway, until after 1845, collective deviations from legally permissible conduct, as in the case of the Hauge and Thrane movements, were most systematically described by investigative agencies that contribute to their repression.

My effort in this chapter to estimate the magnitude and regional distribution of organized lay activism within Norwegian society by 1891 (except for the Dissenter Census of that year) is necessarily based on less systematic sources of evidence. Among these, as we shall see, by far the most useful and important is Ola Rudvin's two-volume history of the Inner-Mission Society, published on the occasion of its one-hundredth anniversary. John Nome's comparable study of the outer-mission society's first hundred years is of more restricted utility for present purposes.[2]

Lay activism and the erosion of clerical control

Clerical control over lay expressions of religiosity within the state church parishes was largely dependent after 1845 upon a traditional interpretation and acceptance of Article XIV in the Augsburg Confession of 1530. The basic principle here was contained in the terms *ritus vocatus*, "rightly called," which defined formal qualifications for leadership in public worship. All clerical generations until 1891 agreed that they alone, through training, ordination, and official appointment to parish posts, met this criterion. Unordained deacons, teachers, and, above all, lay preachers did not meet this qualification, however intense their inner calling or popularly recognized their personal charisma. This fundamental distinction became the most pervasive focus of role-system controversy for the next fifty years.[3] All scholarly efforts to account for regionally variable patterns of lay mobilization and control take this issue as basic to the whole historical process of religious differentiation, when viewed from inside the establishment, without direct reference to underlying political–economic cleavages that intensified during the same period.

Formal control over the educational labor force remained essentially the same during this period. Any teacher who left the state church thereby relinquished his post. Tenure conditions were such that confessional deviations by teachers could be effectively contained until later crises required their participation in the fight against an emergent secularism. The marked over-representation of teachers among Bible Messengers approved for parish action by the clerically dominated executive committee of the Luther Foundation, organized in 1868, points to a reliance on their more predictable Confessional loyalty, if only because of a greater vulnerability to clerical discipline.[4]

The character of professional theological training at the university underwent a period of transition with little discernible ideological impact between the years when Hersleb and Stenersen died (1835 and 1836) and 1849, when Gisle Johnson was appointed to the faculty. By 1850, students in the Hersleb–Stenersen tradition had totally displaced Copenhagen Rationalists at all levels, from bishops to the parish clergy. The heavy impact of Gisle Johnson and his neo-orthodox/Pietist Lutheran Confessionalism upon theological students appears to have been unmatched in the history of Norwegian clerical training, whether in Copenhagen or Oslo. Mannsaaker, on the basis of his exhaustive quantitative study of clerical turnover, has estimated that, by 1875, 70 percent of the clergy had been appointed in the previous twenty years and a large majority of these had studied under Johnson, who used the official qualifying examination as a way of detecting ideological deviants.[5]

The most crucial difference between these two traditions derived from their respective attitudes toward the laity and the Johnsonians' efforts to repress ideological deviation, both among the clergy and within the expanding educational labor force.

Professor Johnson's influence produced a clerical generation that regarded its parishioners as educated, but not yet awakened, Lutherans. While men of the previous generation maintained their traditional status distance, the new pastors, driven by intense missionary zeal, both reduced that distance and altered the content of clergy/laity relationships. They did not, however, unqualifiedly accept lay preaching in violation of their continued commitment to the *ritus vocatus* principle. Willingness to cooperate with lay activists remained contingent on the latter's confessional purity and continued subordination to the clerical office. When *Det Norske Misjonsselskap* was nationally organized in 1842 (on the basis of some previously established parish locals) with a view to training and supporting missionaries for work *outside* Norway, the question of formal ordination of these missionaries proved to be a divisive issue.[6]

The cooperation of Haugean and other lay activists with the clergy was contingent upon their definition of a given pastor's spiritual qualifications. Even if these criteria were satisfied, it did not follow that he became the self-evident leader within a local society. This egalitarian leadership principle was particularly strong in the less sharply stratified dioceses of Bergen and, perhaps to a lesser extent, Agder.

As Norway became a home mission field for the Johnsonian clergy and continued as one for lay activists, Gisle Johnson's role as leader of "his" clergy and guide to the laity issued in an effort to mediate between the contradictory demands of these two groups. The religious literacy gap continued to narrow between university-trained pastors on the one hand and unordained but literate laymen on the other (e.g., seminarians, ex-school teachers, lay preachers, etc.). Claims to special professional competence became increasingly irrelevant to emerging styles of popular religiosity. Ordination, it may be imagined, stood revealed as a liturgical event barren of spiritual meaning when the candidate in question was not himself an awakened Christian, but simply highly trained in intellectual and ritual routines. Given the new clergy's deviation from church-type universalism toward an incipient sect-type spiritual elitism, combined with the fact that many of them were haunted by the ghost of Kierkegaard, their continued claim to a monopoly on public preaching was at best equivocal. That claim was, most simply, based squarely on the very un-Kierkegaardian *ritus vocatus* principle of Article XIV.

The tensions generated by these contradictory expectations could no longer be ignored when, in 1868, Johnson, following a Swedish organizational precedent, led in establishing the Luther Foundation (*Luthersstiftelsen*; hereafter referred to as LF). The objective was to facilitate and control the activities of local Inner-Mission Societies which, beginning at Skein in Lower Telemark in 1853, had appeared at several points throughout the country. The locals established before 1868 appear to have been partly inspired by and modeled upon foreign mission society examples. Indeed, plans for such home mission activities were often initiated at regional and other meetings of that society.

When LF's executive committee in Oslo, with Johnson as chairman, made public its objectives and procedures, it had already been attacked by fourteen out of Oslo's seventeen clergy, with the bishop and diocesan dean as leaders. Their accusation that LF would become a second ministry of church affairs was at least partially vindicated by later developments.[7]

The controversial core of LF's program consisted of the nationwide distribution of religious literature by laymen known as Bible Messengers (*Bibelbud*), who were, in principle, approved by the executive committee in Oslo. The crucial issue, once again, was whether these men would be permitted to preach while distributing tracts. A large majority of the clergy continued to oppose this threat to its prerogatives and warned of its divisive impact upon parish religious life. Lay activists, while recognizing the need for doctrinal controls over such preaching similar to those operative within Haugean circles, insisted upon that freedom initiated by Hauge and legally established in 1842. Gisle Johnson attempted to reduce this source of polarization within the overall revival movement by means of his famous *Nødsprinsip* (Emergency Principle). Briefly, he argued that a church crisis existed which could not be handled by traditional means. The *ritus vocatus* doctrine would have to be temporarily qualified, but not revoked, in order to mobilize lay talents in the fight against indifference, disbelief, incipient sectarianism, dissenter agitation, and other signs of spiritual need.

Regional patterns of lay mobilization as a guide to estimating the magnitude of religious activism: the Luther Foundation, 1868–1894

This strategic expedient failed to satisfy either extreme. The affiliation of local and regional Inner-Mission Societies with LF was contingent upon at least a temporary acceptance of that compromise. Table 3.1, which describes provincial and diocesan variations in the growth of LF affiliates between 1853 and 1891, provides a broadly representative picture of this acceptance pattern. The data arranged in tabular form here were gleaned from Ola Rudvin's enumeration of locals affiliating with and/or contributing to LF, as these were reported at national meetings, usually held at three-year intervals beginning in 1873.[8] Specific founding dates were available for only 77 of the 196 locals affiliated by 1873, twenty years after the first group in Skein and five years after something like centralized records were established in Oslo. Of these, 9 were organized in 1860, 19 between 1861 and 1868, and the remaining 50

Table 3.1. *Inner-mission locals affiliated with or contributing to* Lutherstiftelsen *by time period of establishment, diocese, and province, 1853–1891*

Diocese and province	Total no. of locals, 1853–1873	% of total	1876	1878	1881	1884	1887	1891	Total no. of locals, 1876–1891	% of total	Total no. of locals, 1853–1891	% of total
OSLO (totals)	51	26.0	12	3	6	8	3	22	54	27.4	105	26.7
Akershus	20	10.2	2	2	1	2	1	4	12	6.1	32	8.1
Østfold	17	8.7	2	1	2	3	—	5	13	6.6	30	7.6
Vestfold	10	5.1	3	—	—	2	1	5	11	5.6	21	5.3
Buskerud	4	2.0	5	—	3	1	1	8	18	9.1	22	5.6
HAMAR (totals)	23	11.7	4	4	3	1	3	8	23	11.7	46	11.7
Hedmark	12	6.1	2	1	2	1	1	6	13	6.6	25	6.4
Oppland	11	5.6	2	3	1	—	2	2	10	5.1	21	5.3
AGDER (totals)	75	38.3	21	4	8	3	5	2	44	22.3	119	30.3
Telemark	16	8.2	2	—	—	—	1	1	4	2.0	20	5.1
Aust-Agder	17	8.7	3	—	2	2	1	—	9	4.6	26	6.6
Vest-Agder	25	12.8	11	2	2	—	—	1	16	8.1	41	10.4
Rogaland	17	8.7	5	2	4	1	3	—	15	7.6	32	8.1
BERGEN (totals)	25	12.8	9	1	4	2	19	4	37	18.8	62	15.8
Hordaland	13	6.6	2	1	1	1	4	—	9	4.6	22	5.6
Sogn and Fjordane	6	3.1	2	—	1	1	10	2	16	8.1	22	5.6
Møre and Romsdal	6	3.1	5	—	2	—	5	2	12	6.1	18	4.6

TRONDHJEM (totals)	7	3.6	7	4	3	3	4	2	23	11.7	30	7.6
Sør-Trondelag	3	1.5	3	2	1	—	—	—	6	3.0	9	2.3
Nord Trondelag	4	2.0	4	2	2	3	4	2	17	8.6	21	5.3
TROMSØ (totals)	15	7.7	6	2	2	—	1	6	15	7.6	30	7.6
Nordland	9	4.6	4	2	2	—	1	5	12	6.1	21	5.3
Troms	6	3.1	1	—	—	—	—	1	2	1.0	8	2.0
Finnmark	0	0.0	1	—	—	—	—	—	1	0.5	1	0.3
Total	196	100	59	18	26	17	35	42	196	100	392	100

during the five-year period, 1868–1873. Only 1 of the 9 and 5 of the 19 locals reporting founding dates before 1861 and 1869, respectively, were in rural parishes. If this pattern can be taken as representative for all locals affiliated by 1873, we may conclude that (1) the movement spread from urban to rural areas, and (2) the period of most rapid growth was after the establishment of LF in 1868.

Rudvin estimates that by 1873 there were about 250 local societies rather evenly distributed throughout the country. I have assumed that this figure includes those locals not choosing to affiliate with LF. Given the discrepancy between that total and the 196 locals reported as affiliated by that year, as well as their obviously uneven distribution through the country, this assumption seemed justified. Moreover, in this same context Rudvin cites two major regional associations, one in Lower Telemark with 14 locals, and the other in Hordaland Province with "not less than" 30 locals which explicitly opted for continued independence.[9]

The organizational initiative for this lay-mobilization process appears to have stemmed from one or a combination of levels, local, regional, and national. By 1873, eighteen associations (*fellesforeninger*) had been established, half of them after 1869. In some cases, an association composed of representatives from scattered localities in the area was established first in order to promote the organization of viable locals in the usual sense. In other cases, pre-existing locals formed an association with a view to further organizational work. LF, moving cautiously and with rather meager resources at first, was inclined to leave this activity to such local or regional initiative. An LF emissary and/or Bible Messenger might join this process at some point, but only after it was begun and a specific request was sent to and accepted by the Oslo committee, which tried to avoid sending a man to an area where the clergy was known to be opposed.

Several of these provincial, subprovincial, or urban-area associations sponsored their own lay evangelists, whose activities were not restricted by LF's clerical inhibitions. The number of lay preachers controlled by these associations, in contrast to LF's Bible Messengers, was probably larger at any given time and apparently increased between about 1870 and 1891, when LF explicitly dropped the Emergency Principle and changed its name to The Norwegian Inner-Mission Society. By 1894, Rudvin estimates that about 400 lay preachers were active and, according to the statistical records of that year, 218 men visited locals within their own associational areas, in contrast to only 26 sponsored by the national organization.

The extent to which policy differences between these two organizational levels reflected and/or facilitated religious diversification within the overall home mission itself, as well as Norway's total population, is obviously an empirical question. Numbers are helpful in evaluating this. Rudvin reports that by 1894 there were 420 national affiliates with an average membership of 69, for an aggregate membership of about 28,000. In addition, there were 264 locals for women within the regional associations not included in the above figures. Rudvin's estimate of 69 as the average membership size for the 420 male-dominated locals is based on reports from half of those units. It seems plausible to infer that those not reporting were usually smaller and rural in location.[10]

He provides the range of membership size only for 1873, from 7 women in one rural local to Bergen's enrollment of 598, with an average between 40 and 50 persons. If we can assume that the 250 locals reported for that year included non-affiliates, as well as all women, whether organized separately or not, then total inner-mission mobilization – as defined by formal criteria – came to about 12,500, when accepting 50 as a working estimate of average size.

As we have seen, the 28,000 persons enrolled by 1894 does not include unaffiliated locals, and therefore underestimates national aggregate mobilization. It is not clear from Rudvin's discussion whether the 264 women's societies represented an additional (and not duplicate) membership beyond the "regular" local's aggregate figure. We will return to this problem later.

Table 3.1 includes only those locals linked with LF before the reorganization of 1891, when Johnson's Emergency Principle was finally dropped. This action removed a major block of affiliation for several provincial associations and scattered locals which had taken a more adamant stand on this issue than had those who joined earlier.

The Trondhjem area association, encompassing Sør-Trøndelag, entered the national in 1892 with 78 locals. Only 9 had affiliated under LF's older system. Rudvin little more than touches upon the reasons for this large block of locals from one of Norway's wealthiest and more populous agricultural provinces remaining outside LF until after the reorganization. The relationship appears to have been distant but friendly, which is congruent with that region's sustained reputation for a moderate laicism when measured against the often bitter protests against LF's policies from Lower Telemark and Østfold, as well as a dissentient lay-dominated local in Oslo itself. The Langesundsfjord Inner-Mission Society (Lower Telemark), which had maintained perhaps the most polemical attitude toward LF of any major association in eastern Norway, joined the reconstituted national organization in 1893 with 55 locals. Østfold, Hans Nielsen Hauge's home province, contained two associations which were among the last to affiliate in eastern Norway. Rudvin does not specify the number of locals. Finally, Nordland's association in the southernmost province of north Norway's Tromsø diocese, brought 45 locals into the Oslo-centered national in 1895.[11]

A strong insistence upon local autonomy within provincial associations partially accounts for those reported as affiliated with LF before 1891. Rudvin emphasizes that this did not imply an unqualified acceptance of LF policy, but was rather a short-term strategic decision, prompted, perhaps, by considerations of economy and the greater utility of collective action in pursuit of common goals. Those refusing to join may have been motivated not only by a more sustained skepticism regarding clerical intentions, but simply by technical problems of communication. A railroad line from Oslo through Akershus, Hedmark, and Sør-Trøndelag to Trondhjem was completed in 1877, while sections of it had been opened earlier: Given LF's policy of offering to facilitate and coordinate local and associational initiative rather than attempting futile, if not counter-productive, efforts at control, we may infer that the two northern associations opted for continued autonomy until other crises dictated a collective strategy. The reorientation of 1891 signaled the collapse of clericalism, making affiliation with the Oslo center ideologically acceptable, at least in eastern and southern Norway.

Such willingness to overlook the past was not shared by radical activists, concentrated above all in the West Country province of Hordaland in Bergen diocese. This diocese had an early and sustained tradition of Pietist bishops, as well as a scattering of evangelistic clergy. Hauge had traversed the provinces from Vest-Agder in the southwest to Møre and Romsdal in the northwest before settling in Bergen as a merchant in 1801. It may be suggested, but not fully demonstrated, that Haugeanism sustained a more radical laicism and less accommodating attitude toward unawakened neighbors and spiritually unqualified clergymen in this region than in the eastern dioceses from Oslo to Trondhjem. Elling Eielsen, perhaps the most militant lay preacher in Haugean history, came from Voss in Hordaland, which, together with its provincial capital and diocesan center, Bergen, became the heartland of West Country opposition to Oslo's efforts to mobilize the periphery within a single, unified national inner-mission organization, both before and after 1891.

It is evident from an examination of Table 3.1 that the West Country, defined as ranging from Vest-Agder to Romsdal, was not in unified opposition to LF policies before 1891. Vest-Agder and Rogaland not only were dramatically over-represented among LF affiliates, but also reached a very high level of formal mobilization earlier than any other province. The most immediate explanation for this organizational fertility may be traced to the fact that The Norwegian Mission Society, while aspiring to nationwide mobilization, was actually composed of locals highly concentrated in these two provinces during the years before and after 1842. When the national organization was established in that year, both its headquarters and a center for training missionaries were located in Stavanger.

Vest-Agder had been the major rural exception to Herrnhut Pietism's urban concentration after 1770, when Pastor Bugge of Vanse parish was said to have attracted the laity in half of Listerland to this style of religiosity. Later (*c.* 1798) Hauge reported the parishes between Kristiansand and Stavanger as being particularly receptive to his efforts. The first major cleavages between lay activists, i.e., Haugeans versus Herrnhut Pietists, surfaced here but were sufficiently reduced by 1842 to make possible effective cooperation in forming The Norwegian Mission Society. As a further indicator of greater ideological/experiential religiosity, this area contained the first major anti-Haugean splinter group in the *Staerktroende* (Strong Believers), appearing in 1825 in Bjerkreim, a parish in southern Rogaland, which sustained its existence for several years.

The apparent willingness of many inner-mission locals in these two provinces to go along with LF's equivocal policy before 1891 may reflect their more extensive long-term experience in organizational accommodation, both with the clergy and among lay activists, than elsewhere in the West Country.

It is obviously difficult to estimate the magnitude of lay mobilization within Bergen diocese in the absence of systematic research on the number and distribution of locals which never affiliated with LF. Rudvin provides occasional quantitative clues and impressionistic statements on this problem. The largest and best-known Hordaland association outside of Bergen, encompassing South Hordaland, Hardanger and Voss, established in 1864, had organized 39 locals by 1876, 15 of which had some connection with LF. Eide's less systematic account leaves the impression that initiative, particularly for the coastal area north of Bergen, came from migrants to Bergen, who organized *støtteforening* (support societies) designed to promote local mobilization in their home parishes.[12]

If we assume that the timing and tempo of locals reported from Sogn and Fjordane were at least partially representative of a less visible recruitment pattern, we may infer that this process developed later and showed signs of a drift toward the less militant Oslo center. Combining clues from Rudvin and Eide, together with Gabriel Øidne's historical–ecological analysis of related ideological indicators from 1891,[13] it seems probable that the southern and, above all, coastal parishes of this province were more firmly linked to West Country inner-mission attitudes. Finally, Møre and Romsdal, which was actually divided between the Bergen (Sunn-Møre) and Trondhjem dioceses (Romsdal and Nord-Møre), appears to have split along similar lines, with the more radical, Bergen-oriented activists concentrated in the southern parishes with their center in Aalesund. The northern parishes, in closer and more frequent communication with the Trondhjem association's "friendly scepticism," appears to have shared that attitude toward LF policy, as suggested by the fact that Nord-Møre's Rural Parish Association affiliated with LF in 1892, bringing 8 locals into the national.

Just what the magnitude of West Country mobilization outside the national organization was by 1894 remains problematic, above all in the Bergen diocese from Hordaland to Sunn-Møre. The estimate suggested earlier of 28,000 men as holding formal membership within the national fails to provide an adequate picture of total lay mobilization for the country as a whole. If the Sundhordaland, Hardanger and Voss Association contained 39 locals in 1876, given its reputation for militant organizational work, it seems not un-reasonable to estimate that by 1891 the number had increased to at least 50. Further, if we assume that the other provinces classified here under Bergen diocese contained an additional 50 locals not included in Rudvin's report for 1894, the consequent West Country total of 100 can be used as a crude working estimate for revising the national figure upward. Applying Rudvin's average membership size (69) for LF affiliates to this figure, a total of about 7,000 West Country Dissidents results. Granted the adequacy of this sequence of assumptions and inferences based on fragmentary evidence, it may be suggested that by 1894 national aggregate membership rose to about 35,000 persons, organized in 530 local societies.

This figure may exaggerate formal membership but certainly under-estimates the magnitude of informal allegiance to inner-mission goals and activities. No student of social movements or voluntary associations would limit his or her scope of influence to formal activists. The problem, of course, is what multiplier to use in order to arrive at a persuasive statement. It is probable that such a figure would vary historically and cross-culturally according to demographic and structural conditions, including the age composition, sex ratio, family size, regional variations in social cleavages, and the scope of horizontal mobility within a population.

If we make the crude but least problematic assumption that our 35,000 adults represented about 18,000 households with a minimum average of three children each, then an additional 54,000 persons at least experienced an inner-mission family. Combining these figures, we may conclude that by 1894 about 89,000 individuals lived within the immediate orbit of that movement.

Norwegian dissent: its size, regional distribution, and composition as a comparative point of reference, 1891

A comparison of these inferential "empirical" constructions with a second form of organized religious voluntarism will provide some guidelines for their critical re-examination and at the same time furnish a more adequate basis for an assessment of organized lay activism within a resident population of about 2 million by 1891.

According to the comprehensive dissenter census of 1891, there were 30,658 persons outside the state church.[14] If overt separatism could recruit a population of that size, despite fragmented organizational composition and consequent competition for scarce resources, it then seems most probable that our inner-mission estimate of 35,000 core adults, plus 54,000 children living within the immediate orbit of such influence, is too low. Organizational and logistic contrasts alone would point to this conclusion in view of the Luther Foundation's local, regional, and national network of communication for mobilizing souls and resources. Moreover, as we have seen, passage of the Dissenter Law in 1845 over the opposition of Haugean and other rural opponents provided part of the stimulus for and justification of lay activism within the state church parishes. Despite accelerating tensions between inner-mission militants and the Johnsonian clergy, they remained united in their common opposition to deviations from Lutheran Confessionalism.

Secondly, if legally registered dissent represents the most radical but still "religious" form of popular protest against an established order, then our regional contrasts may be reconsidered in some useful ways in the light of more reliable data. Table 3.2 describes the rural/urban distribution of dissenters by diocese and province. Their massive concentration in Oslo and Agder (notably, Telemark and Aust-Agder) is most immediately apparent, with about 80 percent of the national total recorded from these southeastern-most dioceses.

Some of the more familiar social correlates of this aggregation pattern are the following. First, on a national level, while 23 percent of the population lived within formally defined urban boundaries, 53 percent of all dissenters were urbanites. If we exclude Tromsø diocese, there is a direct rank–order correlation between urbanization and dissent at the diocesan level (see Table 3.3). Oslo diocese, in first place with 28.8 percent of the nation's population, was 43.5 percent urbanized and contained 49.5 percent of all dissenters, while Agder, in the second rank, contained 18.4 per cent of the population, of whom 25.3 percent were urban, with 30.9 percent of all dissenters.

Such reliance on legal urbanism without reference to the geographic

Table 3.2. *Rural/urban distribution of dissenter population by diocese and province in 1891*

Diocese and province	Rural	Urban	Total	%
OSLO (totals)	5,314	9,869	15,183	49.5
Akershus	503	87	590	1.9
Oslo (city)	—	3,974	3,974	13.0
Østfold	1,873	3,082	4,955	16.2
Vestfold	2,080	1,485	3,565	11.6
Buskerud	858	1,241	2,099	6.8
HAMAR (totals)	450	145	595	1.9
Hedmark	289	136	425	1.4
Oppland	161	9	170	0.5
AGDER (totals)	5,726	3,744	9,470	30.9
Telemark	1,780	1,899	3,679	12.0
Aust-Agder	2,665	777	3,442	11.3
Vest-Agder	498	378	876	2.9
Rogaland	783	690	1,473	4.8
BERGEN (totals)	443	1,461	1,904	6.2
Hordaland	386	—	386	1.3
Bergen (city)	—	1,091	1,091	3.6
Sogn and Fjordane	18	2	20	0.1
Møre and Romsdal	39	368	407	1.3
TRONDHJEM (totals)	522	434	956	3.1
Sør-Trondelag	222	396	618	2.0
Nord-Trondelag	300	38	338	1.1
TROMSØ (totals)	1,982	595	2,577	8.4
Nordland	754	82	836	2.7
Troms	1,090	384	1,474	4.8
Finnmark	138	129	267	0.9

Table 3.3. *Diocesan distribution of dissenters and Luther Foundation affiliates as related to aggregate population and urbanization*

Diocese	1891 dissenters (%)	Luther Foundation affiliates		Total population		1891 urban (%)
		by 1873 (%)	by 1891 (%)	1875 (%)	1891 (%)	
OSLO	49.5	26.0	26.7	27.0	28.8	43.5
HAMAR	1.9	11.7	11.7	13.0	11.3	3.8
AGDER	30.9	38.3	30.3	19.3	18.4	25.3
BERGEN	6.2	12.8	15.8	19.8	19.9	18.8
TRONDHJEM	3.1	3.6	7.6	10.9	10.2	14.5
TROMSØ	8.4	7.7	7.6	10.0	11.3	7.5

location of a province or diocese, as well as patterns of population dispersal within them, obscures variations in the extent to which rural populations in these several administrative units were exposed to outside influence. Historically, while relative ease of communication had been characteristic (with variations) of the entire Norwegian coast, the penetration of foreign contacts had been greatest in Østfold and Vestfold generally, as well as the coastal parishes of lower Telemark, Aust-Agder, Vest-Agder, and Rogaland. By this rather simplistic criterion, Hamar diocese was most isolated, with the inland parishes of Bergen and Trondhjem next in order of accessibility. Tromsø, while geographically the most remote of all six dioceses, consisted of an elongated coastal strip with a shallow hinterland, except for Finnmark province. During the late nineteenth century this region had experienced a significant in-migration of surplus population from the provinces farther south. Furthermore, this quasi-colonial area was economically dependent upon mercantile interests in the cities of Bergen and Trondhjem for the marketing of its fish, and in this sense its population was more vulnerable to fluctuations in both national and international markets than the inland parishes of Bergen, Trondhjem, and Hamar dioceses. These factors may account in part for its disproportionately large dissenter population. Broadly speaking, then, these distributive patterns correspond to the relationships found in other times and places between degrees of exposure to outside symbolic resources and the magnitude of dissent.

A comparison of these regional variations with the LF affiliation pattern of inner-mission locals is summarized in Table 3.3. It should be borne in mind when considering these contrasts that the dissenter data refer to individuals and, presumably, are as complete and reliable as many other census enumerations, while the inner-mission figures include only those local societies willing to affiliate with LF before the policy changes of 1891, as derived from Rudvin's archival research on the problem. This means that we are comparing the regional distribution of two extremes within the activist population, i.e., inner-mission accommodators with clear-cut separatists. Given these qualifications, a few more-or-less persuasive contrasts may be observed, based on the three tables presented thus far.

First, it is most evident that LF, with its national territorial organization, penetrated the rural parishes more deeply and systematically than the fragmented and competitive dissenter groups were capable of doing. Secondly, LF mobilization was more evenly distributed throughout the country, as indicated by the closer correspondence between each diocese's share of the national population and the percentage of all LF locals reported as organized within their boundaries by 1891. The radical deviation of Agder diocese (note Rogaland and Vest-Agder) from this correspondence pattern will be examined more closely in due course.

Finally, it seems reasonable to consider some possible connections between the timing and tempo of organizational affiliation with LF and both the relative magnitude and the more specific composition of dissenter populations, focusing only upon some contrasts between the Oslo, Agder, and Bergen dioceses. First, the most sustained and militant East Country opposition to LF's Emergency Principle was concentrated in Oslo (city), Østfold, Lower Telemark, and some parishes of Aust-Agder, where a disproportionate number of the nation's dissenters was located. Affiliation was often delayed, as we have seen, until after the clerical capitulation of 1891. The higher visibility of numerically substantial and often quite "respectable" separatist models may have shaped the bargaining process which characterized the accommodation pattern in these areas. Lay militants could use the threat of organized withdrawals from the state church in order to gain concessions from the opposition.

The single most significant case of such withdrawal began in 1877, when several Lutheran Free Church congregations were organized at scattered points throughout this area and rapidly became the largest dissenter group in Norway, with 8,194 members. Of this total, 6,871 (84%) were located in the Oslo diocese and the two eastern provinces of Agder diocese: Telemark and Aust-Agder. Potentially, this movement was particularly dangerous, since it was initiated by two state-church clergymen who resigned their parish posts in order to establish congregations composed exclusively of "awakened" Lutheran Christians. Theologically, therefore, it did not represent a significant deviation from the views of inner-mission activists within the region. Sociologically, it was more separatist than dissenting. It has remained the only sizeable group outside the state church to have originated within Norway.[15]

The earliest non-Lutheran dissenters began their modest inroads during the 1850s. By 1891 the largest of these were the Methodists (8,187), Baptists (4,228), and Roman Catholics (1,004). On another plane, 5,095 persons were reported as outside the church without having affiliated with any organized religious group. These five census categories accounted for 87 percent of all dissenters (26,708). A few comments on the Methodists' distribution and its implications will suffice here. First, while the Methodists almost precisely matched the Free Church membership, the rural/urban location of the two groups was exactly reversed, as follows:

	Rural	*Urban*
Free Church	5,297	2,897
Methodists	2,745	5,442

This contrast in rural penetration is congruent with our earlier observation regarding the relative capacity of the inner mission and dissenters to establish themselves outside urban centers, given the strong Lutheran Confessionalism of the Free Church. On the other hand, Methodists were slightly less concentrated in the areas from Aust-Agder through Oslo diocese than were Free Church adherents, with 76.7 percent versus 85 percent resident in this region.

Finally, the relative rapidity with which the two bodies reached their 1891 level of membership is worth noting. The Methodists, beginning in 1853, had become the largest dissenter group in Norway by 1875, with 2,775 membership, increasing most rapidly thereafter until 1891 when the tempo of growth began to decline. The Free Church attracted its slightly larger number of adherents during the shorter fourteen-year period, 1877 to 1891, and continued to grow thereafter at a faster rate than the Methodists.

Einar Molland has asserted that the Methodists were usually viewed with much greater good will by state-church authorities than other separatist societies and that in reality their style of religiosity was very close to that of ordinary Norwegian "awakened" Christianity.[16] It may be that the earlier Herrnhut Pietist inroads in the Oslo fjord area facilitated their acceptance, in view of some common historical antecedents. However this may have been, the fact that over 50 percent of all Norwegian dissenters were organized within

Free Church and Methodist congregations suggests a greater symbolic congruence with established modes of religious expression in these provinces.

In conclusion, we may infer that the inner-mission unity finally realized here was facilitated by the absorption and containment of "extremists" in these and still other groups, with their variable degrees of dissent, as well as an experienced need for a more unified response to their challenge.

The timing and tempo of organizational affiliation with LF in Vest-Agder and Rogaland, as noted above, were dramatically different. Affiliation there began early, remained rather steady, and reached greater magnitude, both absolutely and relatively, than it did in any of the other provinces in Norway, while their share of the dissenter population was remarkably low. This latter point is particularly surprising in view of the fact that these provinces were not only more urbanized than most (27.5 % in 1891) but that they had experienced some of the earliest and most dramatic episodes of lay-movement factionalism and dissenter agitation in Norway before 1845. By 1891, with 9.7 percent of Norway's population, they contained 18.5 percent of LF's affiliates and 7.7 percent of all dissenters. Table 3.4 describes the relative size of the four largest dissenter categories within our three regions, compared with their proportions in the national population. Norwegian Quakers, whose fight for religious liberty contributed more to the passage of dissenter legislation than any other single group, were overwhelmingly concentrated in Rogaland and Vest-Agder, with 216 out of 231 reported from these provinces.[17]

The relative ease and tranquility of organizational fusion here between 1868 and 1891 may be partially traceable to its earlier confrontation with and resolution of religious factionalism, as indicated, above all, by the reconciliation of differences between Haugeans, Pietists, and a few state-church clergymen, as expressed institutionally in The Norwegian Mission Society. The process of lay mobilization and organizational accommodation implied here preceded passage of the Dissenter Law by three years. When, twenty-six years later, the Luther Foundation initiated a comparable effort to coordinate and expand the activities of local and regional inner-mission societies, its growth rate in these two provinces became remarkable. It was made possible not only by this pre-existent organizational structure. The sustained period of clergy/laity cooperation experienced here, while certainly not free from conflict, had meant that both the level of clerical resistance to lay autonomy and, reciprocally, the intensity of lay hostility to clerical pretensions were lower here than in the eastern provinces discussed below, when LF appeared on their respective scenes in 1868. The explanatory value of these and other regional contrasts will be refined and expanded in chapter 5.

Finally, Bergen diocese, which remained the heartland of national oppo-

Table 3.4. *Relative magnitude of five census dissenter categories within three regions compared with each other and the national distribution*

Dissenter category	Oslo diocese Telemark and Aust-Agder (%)	Vest-Agder and Rogaland (%)	Bergen diocese (%)	National proportions (%)
Free Church	30.8	30.7	4.4	26.7
Methodists	28.2	21.8	41.0	26.7
No affiliation	15.7	24.2	11.0	16.6
Baptist	10.1	3.7	18.0	13.8
Quakers	—	9.2	—	—
Total	84.8	89.7	74.4	83.8

sition to the Oslo center for decades after 1891, reported an even smaller (6.2 %) share of all dissenters than the two southwest provinces (7.7 %). Over half of these were located in the city of Bergen itself. Methodists and Baptists were over-represented, while Free Church adherents were under-represented among them. Bergen's greater isolation, in contrast to Oslo and Agder diocese, was due not only to its location and lower level of urbanization (18.8 %), but the greater concentration of that urban population in a smaller number of centers. Bergen's rural parishes reported the smallest dissenter population of Norway's six diocesan units. It would appear that despite this region's reputation for radical laicism, as indicated organizationally by the militant stand of the powerful Sundhordaland, Hardanger, and Voss Association, such protest, with its incipient separatist overtones, seldom went beyond the limits of Pontoppidan Confessionalism, at least as defined by West Country activists.

The Norwegian Mission Society: some fragmentary evidence regarding its probable magnitude

Our final, major source of quantitative evidence regarding organized religious activism in Norway between 1850 and 1891 derives from John Nome's basic work on the organizational growth of foreign mission societies during this period. Representatives from 65 already existing locals were present at the Stavanger meeting in 1842, where the national society was to have both its headquarters and a training school for missionaries. Popular support at this early stage in its development was concentrated in Rogaland and Vest-Agder, but also ranged from Arendal in the east to Bergen in the west. Twenty-seven years later, in 1870, 677 locals were contained within the national organization. By 1884 there were 830 parish locals and about 1,700 women's societies contributing to outer-mission efforts.[18]

It is remarkable that a phenomenon of this magnitude should be alluded to so casually by both church and social historians, particularly in view of the claim that modern Norwegians contribute more per capita to foreign missions than do any other people in the world. Possibly, since the missionary work took place outside Norway, their evangelistic efforts were so vicarious and far removed as to be, by definition, less obtrusive than in the case of inner-mission activists. Their activities were also less consequential for internal church politics, including laity/clergy conflicts over public styles of religious expression and control.

As we have seen, the earliest plans for home-mission organization were often initiated at regional and national meetings of this older and more established society. While there is some evidence of competition for the allocation of resources between outer- and inner-mission objectives, no really sustained conflicts apparently worthy of detailed historical discussion developed. The extent to which membership in the two movements overlapped is unknown but is generally regarded as having been very high, particularly, perhaps, in Vest-Agder and Rogaland. Nevertheless, given the simple numerical contrast in the number of locals affiliated with the two societies, it is obvious that by 1884 foreign concerns mobilized broader support than the home mission "alternative" reached ten years later.

Nome, while providing graphs showing aggregate monetary contributions to the national society between 1842 and 1942, does not provide enough information to make a systematic comparison with home-mission patterns of regional and temporal recruitment possible. Moreover, just what the average membership size and sex-ratio composition of the 830 parish societies was can only be constructed, once again, on the basis of some plausible assumptions and inferences without the more systematic empirical checks provided by Rudvin. If we assume that these societies were devoted primarily to generating financial and other resources in support of missionary training and field activities, their formal membership may have been smaller than that of inner-mission locals, composed, presumably, of awakened parishioners primarily concerned with increasing their numbers. On the other hand, it seems highly probable that the aggregate number of individuals contributing to but not recorded as members of outer-mission societies was much larger than the corresponding inner-mission category of sympathetic, but otherwise passive, friends.

We may imagine that participating in, and/or contributing to, foreign missions provided, as it were, a sense of vicarious piety which was social-psychologically less expensive than defining fellow parishioners as spiritual somnambulists whom you are required to awaken through more direct and personal action. Inner-mission activities were, by definition, divisive, implying a spiritual elitism approximating that of sectarian movements. When The Norwegian Mission Society celebrated its fiftieth anniversary in 1892, its less obtrusive respectability was established. It had become an aspect of parish life which the new clergy and their wives could participate in and promote without feeling directly challenged on their home ground. Contrariwise, the inner mission was unable to achieve full national integration, even after publicly repudiating the *ritus vocatus* principle, which had been the major confessional basis for distinguishing the parish clergy from ambulatory lay preachers. All this is not to say that the first fifty years of outer-mission mobilization was free of clergy/laity conflicts over a wide range of issues, including their respective control prerogatives within the movement.[19] These conflicts, however, were never as intense and regionally divisive as those within the home mission. By the late 1870s, the routinization of conflict was facilitated by a generational shift in leadership within both parties to the controversy, which issued in an essentially democratic but church-oriented polity within the movement.

It follows from these and other contrasts that the foreign mission's organizational network could be related to the parish system without as much strain on traditional role expectations. While a similar process of mutual cooperation was under way between the inner-mission movement and the clergy, its progress was so politicized by nonreligious social and regional cleavages that a comparable level of organizational efficiency and mobilizing power could not be sustained. Returning to the question of relative magnitude, both empirical evidence (number of locals) and these *systemic* contrasts suggest that by 1884 foreign mission advocates, but not necessarily organized activists, surpassed the level achieved by their inner-mission counterparts ten years later by at least two to one. Given the time error built into the ratio (i.e., 1884/1894), the consequent distortion understates the relative size of the two movements. That is, by 1894 the ratio was greater than two to one. We will return to this problem later. The number of women's societies mentioned by Nome (1,700) and Rudvin (264) pose a difficult problem in this connection. If we assume that they represented, as it were, independently organized sewing-circle subgroups whose membership was composed primarily of the same women enrolled in the larger, male-dominated parish locals rather than fully segregated units whose membership was actually reported separately, we may be in danger of underestimating the magnitude of mobilization within the two movements. Obviously, these are not mutually exclusive possibilities. Nevertheless, the greater plausibility of "subgroup relationship" is suggested by the following.

Nome, who devotes more attention to these organizations and their activities than does Rudvin, leaves the clear impression that they were usually small enough to constitute intimate work circles producing household goods (e.g., clothing) for direct contribution or sale, with the proceeds going to the cause.[20] Devotional activities, while certainly present, were secondary to these more instrumental goals. It seems probable that inner-mission women's groups engaged in similar activities and were of comparable size. If this line of reasoning is sound, then an average size of 10 women may be suggested as a crude working estimate. Accepting this figure as our multiplier, we can infer that by 1884 about 17,000 women were engaged in foreign-mission support and that by 1894, 2,640 women formally affiliated with the reorganized national inner-mission movement were contributing their skills to its goals.

The remarkable difference in the relative number of these units within the two organizations must be considered before constructing an estimate of overall foreign-mission membership. To support the training and field work of foreign missionaries required an outlay of hard currency several times greater than that needed by ambulatory lay preachers or Bible Messengers evangelizing their home populations. In point of fact, modest efforts to train or compensate these seasonal workers, who constituted the backbone of inner-mission efforts, were strongly resisted by radical activists who viewed such practices as unscriptural and anti-Haugean. These men, who were supposed to live for and not off the gospel, were more often than not supported in much the same fashion that ambulatory school teachers had been before the educational labor force was gradually transformed after 1860.

Expressed in the language of economists, foreign-mission enterprise was capital-intensive, trying to operate within an overall economy struggling with the problems of primitive capitalist accumulation in order to monetize the exchange system and build the infrastructure (e.g., railroads) required for a developing market economy. On the other hand, inner-mission enterprise was labor-intensive, requiring much smaller initial outlays of capital where production consisted largely of printing tracts which could be distributed through a quasi-subsistence pattern of exchange.

Viewed from this perspective, the relative number of ladies' societies contributing to the support of outer- (1,700) and inner-mission (264) enterprises becomes a function of their respective needs for capital investment. Further, in addition to the motivational contrasts constructed earlier, we may imagine that foreign-mission units of capital accumulation had an advantage in whatever competition may have existed for the recruitment of this unpaid labor force. Simply stated, the vicarious conversion of one's heathen brethren is not only a source of joy derived from obligations fulfilled but also provides a sense of communion with the exotic, larger world of human kind. Moreover, some variant on the principle of perceived relative deprivation operated here in the allocation of scarce resources between outer- and inner-mission objectives. After all, a kind of spiritual infrastructure for the production of educated Christians had long been established in Norway through parish school education and traditional church life. Surely the provision of similar opportunities for those less fortunate could easily claim first priority in the minds of that larger segment of the Norwegian population less inclined to perceive domestic spiritual needs as having reached the crisis stage implied by Professor Johnson's Emergency Principle.

Haugean policies regarding the role of women in devotional life were much more egalitarian and activist than had been the case for the larger population, and this view was at least partly shared by inner- and outer-mission advocates. The problem here is not whether women were included in male-dominated parish locals. They were present as nonvoting members of these less instrumental and more devotional "policy-making" units. The question at issue is the extent to which the same women held dual membership in both types of societies, or did they constitute additional membership to be taken into consideration in estimating the magnitude of organized lay activism. In the absence of direct empirical evidence, the subgroup, dual membership assumption seems most plausible. The two-to-one ratio (1,700/830) of these two types within The Norwegian Mission Society by 1884, granted our "sewing circle" estimate averaging ten women per local, seems to point in this direction.

Just why the corresponding inner-mission ratio (430/264) should be almost but not quite the reverse is more problematic. As already indicated, Rudvin devotes very little attention to ladies' locals as such. Moreover, the issue is further complicated by the fact that it was not always possible to distinguish between outer- and inner-mission societies composed of women, since both on occasion contributed to the Luther Foundation. If this practice was very common, it would go a long way toward explaining both the remarkable difference in the reported number of women's units within the two societies and the reversed ratio within LF, even without reference to their respective needs for capital investment.

Assuming dual membership, what figure can we propose as approximating the magnitude of formal, adult mobilization within The Norwegian Mission Society by 1891? Obviously, the number of locals did not remain at 830 after 1884. Nome estimates that between 1870 and 1884 an average of 10 to 15 societies were established each year. If this tempo continued during the succeeding seven years, a minimum of 70 and a maximum of 105 new locals were affiliated by 1891. Adopting the most conservative figure, there were at least 900 societies in existence by that time; this figure may be used as a basis for further calculations.

I have suggested that the average size of these units was smaller than their inner-mission counterparts, which Rudvin places at 69 in 1894. This proposal stemmed from an assumption regarding their distinctive, primary objectives. That is, home mission locals were first of all concerned with increasing the number of awakened Christians within their own parish areas, while a significant criterion of success for outer-mission societies was the amount of financial support generated by their efforts for evangelistic activities outside the country. The implication here is that effective fund-raising need not require or inspire a large *formal* membership within an organization having this as one of its major objectives. Secondly, as the number of locals increased beyond the absolute number of parishes within Norway, a deliberate process of organizational fission may have developed which created a larger number of smaller, more effective and accessible foreign-mission units.

Specifying an average size, however plausible the above argument may be, necessarily remains a highly arbitrary process. Nevertheless, let us assume a working average of 50 persons per unit, which issues in an estimate of 45,000 activists organized within The Norwegian Mission Society by 1891. There is obviously no way of knowing how many separate households this figure represents. Such activism, unlike traditional parish participation, may very well have led to nuclear and extended family tensions where, for example, both husband and wife were not participants. This demonstrably did occur within the Hauge movement, but with unknown frequency. Given the motivational contrasts constructed earlier, such tensions were more likely to be generated by inner- than outer-mission activist households. Comments by Nome as well as comparative historical inference would suggest that women were more numerous than men in these organizations. Nevertheless, our least problematic procedure is to assume husband and wife membership as the most common pattern. If we assume that the conjectural 45,000 adults represented about 23,000 households with a minimal average of 3 children each, then about 69,000 additional persons lived within the immediate orbit of The

Norwegian Mission Society's influence, giving a combined total of 114,000 persons by 1891.

Finally, in view of the fact that many of the same persons belonged to both inner- and outer-mission societies, how can we "correct" for this overlap in order to construct a final estimate of organized lay activism within the Norwegian State Church by about 1891? There is obviously no empirically verifiable solution to this problem in the absence of membership lists. Perhaps the least problematic solution would be simply to propose a 50 percent overlap based on the two-to-one ratio in number of locals in existence about 1891, i.e., 900 outer- and 530 inner-mission societies. We have noted some of the more obvious errors built into both these figures, most of which point to the probability that they underestimate the actual numbers. Given this overlap assumption, we may infer that about 60,000 adult activists were mobilized in the overall mission movement, representing 30,000 households with 90,000 children. In conclusion, then, about 150,000 Norwegians lived within the immediate orbit of these organizations by 1891.

Conclusion

Organized departures from traditional religious routines in Norwegian society between 1850 and 1891 ranged along a continuum of internal factionalism and external tension, with an established order which conditioned the magnitude of active participation as well as the scope of informal influence. As we go from the most reliable data on dissenters to our empirically based, but logically constructed estimates of inner- and outer-mission activism, we also move along a scale of "societal penetration" from low to high. These three styles of awakened religious expression impinged directly on the inner lives of some 180,000 Norwegian men, women and children living within the immediate orbit of their influence. This estimate, if taken seriously, would mean that by 1891 about 8.5 percent of the total population were either awakened (organized adult activists) or keenly aware of the need for such an experience (children within activist households). Obviously, since this figure is based on our organizational indicators of religious differentiation, it excludes those segments of the awakened laity that found expression either in smaller organizations unaffiliated with these larger ones or that lived out their spiritual lives in more autonomous ways.

Conventional historical descriptions of religious awakenings are understandably vague and lend themselves to dramatic exaggeration. It has been said, for example, that Hans Nielsen Hauge converted Norway to Christianity, while Saint Olaf and Martin Luther, as it were, simply prepared the ground. If this is taken to mean that, building on Pontoppidan's implied criteria of religiosity, Hauge diffused an awareness of the individualistic implications of Lutheranism which were later institutionalized within the overall mission movement, such a statement might be taken seriously.

It should, by now, be obvious that to be aware is not to be awakened. Clearly, the vast majority of Norwegians, perhaps 90 percent according to (our) calculations, remained educated but not awakened Christians, as defined by their activist neighbors and the Johnsonian clergy. As we have seen, these experiential demands constituted a divisive challenge to traditional conceptions of the parish community and the individual's sense of religious identity.

The bedrock of popular religiosity since the conversion from paganism had been and continued to be universal participation in life-cycle ritual occasions administered by the clergy for a passive laity. This mode of religious expression was a matter of public record maintained by the parish clergy in its role as vital statistics collector for the central government, including the ministry of church and education. Baptism, confirmation (after 1740), marriage, and burial by the state-church pastor were obligatory for the entire population until after 1845, when dissenters were exempted.

The only significant effort to make participation in these ceremonial high points voluntary came from the Johnsonian clergy, whose legally prescribed duties forced them to marry individuals they knew to be, at best, educated Christians. They hoped to exploit popular emotional investment in these occasions as an evangelistic device by making conversion a prerequisite for participation. This attempt to gain discretionary power over their administration of selected ritual occasions was part of a larger plan to reform church organization from above so as to gain greater autonomy for the clergy *vis-à-vis* both the state structure and the passive and activist laity. The most organized, articulate resistance to these proposals came from lay activists who, while committed to church reform, wanted it carried through from below in ways that would have been, perhaps, even more spiritually discriminatory. The confrontation here was between opposing conceptions of church polity and not criteria of religiosity. As we have seen, essentially the same dispute within outer- and inner-mission societies issued in final victory for the activist laity.

The implications of these reform proposals for distributions of power and freedom of religious expression could hardly be ignored by politicians responsive to an electorate, even before the introduction of universal male suffrage after 1891. The fact that no structural changes of any significance were made between 1845 and 1891 testifies to the political impotence of both the Johnsonian clergy and, to a lesser extent, awakened segments of the laity who were aligned against them during the parliamentary crises before and shortly after 1884. Those changes which were made, from revocation of the Conventicle Act (1842) to the opening of parish churches to lay speakers (1888) and mission society meetings (1889) did not infringe directly upon the vast majority's right to continue its passive participation in religious life.[21]

Descriptions of church attendance in the nineteenth century are necessarily impressionistic, since, unlike the case of life-cycle ritual occasions, there was no practical value in maintaining a record. Around 1814, according to Molland, church attendance was lowest in cities and East Country rural areas and significantly higher in western and northern regions. Given the distribution and occupant capacity of parish churches as related to population growth and distribution, anything like weekly attendance for a majority of the laity was simply out of the question. These physical limitations were further magnified by the increasing laity/clergy ratio, which reached its high point in 1855 with 3,164 inhabitants for every ordained pastor legally qualified to conduct the traditional Sunday service. When, as Molland writes, churches were *sprengt* (filled to the bursting point)[22] during high points of the Johnsonian awakening, it remained a practical impossibility for this greater attendance to involve more than an increased minority of the population on a regular basis. Nevertheless, whatever the frequency or magnitude of church attendance may have been, it remained overwhelmingly the dominant form of recurrent religious expression among the laity. As inner-mission activists began to build prayer houses (*bedehus*) throughout the country, attendance in them supplemented, but did not displace, participation in parish church services.

4. Elite literacy and styles of religious expression

The range and content of symbolic resources in terms of which alternative life orientations were partially articulated expanded most rapidly after 1860, as new situations disrupted old expectations at an accelerated pace. The interplay between formal educational experience and styles of religious expression, whether awakened, educated and/or secular, continued to vary according to strata and region. Evidence for these plausible assertions remains fragmentary. My objective in this and the following chapter will be to collate and interpret some of the available data bearing on: (1) *elite* literacy, educational experience, and styles of religious expression and (2) in chapter 5, certain changes in the social organization and content of *mass* literacy production in *rural* areas, including some regional contrasts. These variations will be related to the patterns of lay mobilization described in chapter 3, with a view to exploring some possible linkages between them.

The four levels of social stratification distinguished by Dagfinn Mann-saaker in his study of the Norwegian clergy provides a particularly concise and coherent framework within which the most crucial variables shaping these relationships may be described.[1] His classification is based on three major criteria: (1) occupation, including the levels of formal education required to gain access; (2) the amount and source of income from property or work; (3) what he terms "socio-political status," a close equivalent to Max Weber's concept of power. Historically, these are differentially relevant to the rank ordering within and between three types of life situation: (1) the *embettsstand*, a hierarchy of civil and religious officials at the national, provincial, and local levels; (2) urban mercantile and craft activities; (3) the numerically dominant population group engaged in, or deriving their income from, farming, fishing, and/or forestry.

The four strata issuing from these considerations may be outlined and briefly distinguished as follows. First, the highest stratum was composed of top officials in the *embettsstand*, large-scale capitalists and estate owners (*godseigarar*). Just below this was a second, larger and less homogenous stratum composed of other subordinate officials within the *embetsstand*:

substantial bourgeois (*solide borgerar*) and large land-owners (*storbønder*). It is probable that these two strata in combination constituted no more than about 10 percent of the total population at any time during the nineteenth century. Estate owners and large farmers were concentrated in the East Country dioceses of Oslo, Hamar, and Trondhjem. They composed a rural elite with significant, though variable, control over employment opportunities for landless laborers as well as tenure conditions for tenant farmers. Large capitalists and substantial bourgeois, including professionals, constituted a rather mixed urban economic elite which, particularly in the first case, transcended a local base in terms of international or regional trade as well as investments in forest and fishing enterprise. Finally, the most homogeneous segment of these upper strata, the *embetsstand*, based its status claims upon university education and official power, civil and religious. Unlike the regional or urban concentration of large land-holders and merchants, they were obviously more evenly distributed around the country, with the top officials concentrated in Oslo and provincial capitals.

Fluctuating conflicts of interest within and between segments of these upper strata, as well as growing pressures from below, were expressed in shifting political economic cleavages and coalitions which issued in significant redistributions of power, particularly after 1833.[2] As we have seen, the progressive decline in clerical control over laicized styles of religious expression was an integral part of this process. In like manner, major restructuring of the rural parish school system, including curricular expansion, improved training, and growing autonomy of teachers *vis-à-vis* the clergy, which will occupy much of our attention in this and the following chapters, was even more constrained and channeled by these struggles for social power.

The historical visibility of Mannsaaker's two lower strata increased sporadically before 1850, as in the Hauge and Thrane movements, including those segments of his third stratum economically qualified for participation in the political process either as Storting representatives or as members of those communal councils (*Herradsraad*) introduced by the local government act of 1837. Their most sustained visibility accelerated after 1845 in the massive emigration to America and internal migration to urban centers, some of the consequences of which will be touched upon later.

Mannsaaker's third and largest stratum, composed of lower official functionaries (e.g., teachers and bailiffs), petty bourgeois (*smaaborgarar*), and small farmers may be distinguished from his lowest stratum of tenant farmers (*husmenn*) and agricultural and urban workers primarily in terms of their *relatively* high though variable levels of personal autonomy, *vis-à-vis* representatives of the upper strata. As we have seen in chapter 2 and will reconsider below, the social–psychological structure and content of dependency relationships within and between these strata varied regionally in ways which proved highly consequential for the interplay between mass educational development and popular styles of religious expression.

If the dissolution of religious unity in nineteenth-century Norwegian society contained both secularizing and awakening trends, it is evident that neither was randomly distributed in social space. Signs of secularization were most apparent in Mannsaaker's first, second, and fourth strata, particularly in the East country dioceses of Oslo and Hamar. As we have seen and will explore further here, organized activism tended to be concentrated in the third stratum.

The expansion and differentiation of educational experience occurred at all levels. It remained, however, a split-level system until after 1891, in that the school reforms of 1860 failed to institute structural continuity between massive "primary" education in the modern sense and the system of "secondary" education required as a prerequisite for admission to the university. This two-tier system reflected and reinforced a fundamental cleavage in styles of life between those strata popularly labeled as *de kondisionerte* (cultured classes) and *de allmue* (the commonality or common people). Broadly speaking, the former corresponds to the first and second strata, while the latter encompasses those within the two lower strata.

The major descriptive interpretive task of chapters 4 and 5 will be to sketch religious and educational profiles of these strata with special reference to selected contrasts in their changing relationships with pastors, teachers, and lay preachers.

Elite educational experience and styles of religious expression

Initial encounters

Confirmation as a universal rite of passage and the continued use of some variations on Pontoppidan's *Explanation of the Catechism* in preparation for that occasion constituted a shared point of reference for all children, whatever their social or regional origin. The social and symbolic context of that experience was, as we have seen, differentiated according to life situations. Given the urban concentration of the upper strata, their encounters with Pontoppidan were by definition outside the ambulatory system and constituted only part of a more extended and varied educational experience. As to the rural elite of estate owners, officials, and large land-holders, certain probable contrasts in their relationship to the ambulatory system and its limitations may be suggested. Estate owners could and did hire private tutors for the basic education of their children and/or sent them to urban areas for their schooling.[3] Secondly, it is highly probable that a disproportionate number of children from the homes of rural officials attended fixed, rather than ambulatory, schools, since these were usually located (before 1860) near the main parish church and parsonage, where their homes may have been concentrated. As we shall see below, these schools were most likely to be conducted by deacons and, later, seminarians, who were superior to their ambulatory counterparts in both training and experience. Finally, insofar as large land-holders were dependent upon the ambulatory system, their position was a privileged one in that the parish teacher was likely to assemble children in their own homes for more extended periods of time and to stand in a more clearly subordinated position to them while doing so.

The language of Pontoppidan's text, while variably alien to lower strata generally and the rural population in particular, was, if not identical with, at least more familiar to the children of these elites, with the probable exception of some large land-holders. As a consequence, their encounters with Pontoppidan were more likely to facilitate rather than inhibit the acquisition of reading skills, as often happened in the case of children not so advantaged.

Elite educational experience and the clergy

These status-determined contrasts in a child's initial educational experiences, while an integral part of the split-level system, were not its most decisive features. Confirmation terminated formal schooling for a vast majority of the rural population as well as for lower-status groups in urban areas. Almost by definition, what distinguished the elite from commoners was their more sustained exposure to a literate culture which transcended parochial worlds. Their primary, rather than terminal, schooling prepared some of them for, among other alternatives, the gymnasium and the official examination required for admission to the university.

Reference to this advanced educational system has been limited thus far to the state-church clergy, whose pivotal power position not only shaped parish school developments and limited lay activism but also constituted the single most crucial role-system link between these two symbolic worlds. As we have seen, its formal control over popular styles of religious expression began to decline most visibly after 1850. On the other hand, the clergy's relationship to its status peers and superiors had long been more one of being controlled than controlling.

The incipient secularization of Norwegian elite culture in the late eighteenth century continued after 1814, assuming not only intellectual but more "objective" social–historical forms.[4] That is to say, a crucial dimension of this process derived from significant changes in the clergy's *relative* standing *within* the upper strata as indicated by: (1) the differentiation of Norway's professional labor force and the higher educational system required for its production; and (2) a shift downward in the social origins of the clergy, particularly after 1850.

The origins and the training and career patterns of public and private professionals have been described and analyzed more fully than any other segment of the Norwegian population in the nineteenth century. Gross changes in the clergy's prominence within this labor force can be quickly summarized. First, while the number of ordained pastors increased from 400 to 700 between 1815 and 1895, legal professionals multiplied from 329 to 2,000 during the same period, having surpassed the clergy by 1844 with 800 lawyers as opposed to 450 pastors. Concurrently, the percentage of lawyers employed in the public sector (e.g., central and local administration) declined from 69.4 percent to 34.1 percent, as political–economic developments provided a demand for their normative skills in the private sector. The number of medical doctors increased more slowly, from 160 in 1815 to 910 in 1895, while the percentage in public employment declined from 50.7 to 29.[5]

Vilhelm Aubert and others have interpreted these changes as a partial indicator of, among other things, the secularization of higher education. A somewhat similar inference regarding trends in secondary education may be drawn from Tore Lindbekk's work on the training backgrounds of teachers in *gymnasier* and *realskoler* during the nineteenth century.[6] The changing prominence of university graduates in theology is most crucial here. They constituted the single largest group within this modest educational labor force until the late 1840s, when the number of positions began to increase rapidly. From a high point of 39.5 percent of these teachers in 1844, their presence declined to 21.5 percent and then 14.8 percent in 1875 and 1900 respectively. University-trained philologists, who had usually ranked a close second before 1850, sustained their relative dominance thereafter, increasing from 44.5 percent to 54.2 percent of all such positions between 1856 and 1875. Finally, *realister* (natural scientists), who first appear in Lindbekk's table in 1875 with 19.9 percent, constituted 25.1 percent of the total by 1900.[7]

The social recruitment of these teachers and their students gradually expanded downward during the century to include an increasing representation from Mannsaaker's third stratum. Lindbekk reports that the absolute number of teachers in four distinct types of secondary schools was probably less than 100 in 1820 and no more than about 145 in 1837. Thereafter, their numbers expanded rapidly to 1,300 in 1879 and 1,447 in 1900. Only a small minority of these teachers was employed in the upper-level *gymnas*, graduation from which constituted a major, though not exclusive, gateway to university matriculation. For example, in 1890–1891, of 1,572 full-time secondary school teachers 81 taught in a gymnasium. Correspondingly, during the same year, while 18,656 pupils were experiencing some kind of secondary education only 675 were enrolled in a gymnasium.[8] Finally, as Semmingsen indicates, the number of students actually passing the *student-eksamen*, whatever their preparation for it may have been, "remained relatively stable: between 75 and 100 pupils passed every year. In the 1860s the rise began. The numbers reached their first peak in the first half of the 1880s with more than 300 successful candidates per year."[9]

It is evident from these few indicators that some kind of secondary educational experience had been extended beyond the school-age population of the urban (and rural) elite to include a sizeable, though still disproportionately low, representation from the upper, urban segments of Mannsaaker's third stratum. Just what consequences these expanding experiences may have had for styles of religiosity is obviously more problematic. If we assume that university-trained theologians were more likely to reinforce orthodox orientations than were secondary-school teachers, we might infer that as their relative numbers declined, the influence of secular alternatives was more likely to prevail.

Given our concern with the social distribution and magnitude of the Johnsonian revival, it is certainly worth noting that their decline *preceded* Professor Johnson's years of most effective influence upon theological training, and that at least on this dimension his impact was likely to have been constrained.

There is one source of evidence which enables us to say something about the timing and tempo of advanced literacy production and its consequences as an outcome of both secondary and, less certainly, mass educational developments after 1860. This consists of a comprehensive and presumably exhaustive historical bibliography tracing the numerical growth and subject-matter differentiation of Norwegian periodicals from before 1800 until 1920. A thorough utilization of this material would constitute a major undertaking in historical content analysis. Nevertheless, a few of the more salient trends may be cited here. Harold Tveteraas summarizes his findings in a table which describes the decade-by-decade increase of periodicals within twenty subject-matter categories.[10] First, the absolute number of items in all categories rose sharply from 87 published between 1861 and 1870 to 152 during the following

Table 4.1. *Growth and differentiation of Norwegian periodical literature by subject-matter categories, 1861–1900 (absolute numbers)*

Subject-matter category	1861–1870	1871–1880	1881–1890	1891–1900
Mixed content	37	57	77	90
Religion	18	39	55	82
Social questions	5	13	34	42
Agriculture	3	6	18	25
Commerce	5	2	12	19
Other 15 groups	19	35	38	56
Total	87	152	234	314

decade. This accelerated tempo continued during the 1880s and 1890s, increasing from 234 to 314 respectively. A growth rate of this magnitude, while partially attributable to improvements in printing technology and general economic expansion, presupposes a dramatic enlargement of the literate market. Tveterass's second largest category consists of 486 items appealing to a specifically religious market, ranging from diverse theological journals to sectarian publications. On the other hand, he has omitted some 90 local parish publications (*menighetsblad*),[11] most of which began to appear after 1900. His third largest group contained 308 periodicals devoted to the discussion of "social questions" of diverse sorts. Of the remaining 784 titles, 468 were classified in four audience categories as follows: agriculture, household arts, and fishing (139); commerce and communication (148); technical, industrial, and crafts (98); and pedagogy, teacher, or student publications (83). Finally, the residue of 321 items is scattered among the remaining 13 categories in his table. With some exceptions, representations within each of these appear later than the three largest groups and increase most notably after 1860.

Table 4.1 provides some indication of the expansion and differentiation of the periodical market between 1861 and 1900. The five largest categories mentioned above are presented separately, with the remaining fifteen simply aggregated by way of providing a partial profile of higher educational achievement and reader interests during this period. It is my impression from Tveteraas's introduction that the mortality rate of these periodicals was very high, the vast majority continuing in publication for less than a decade. Furthermore, in the absence of anything like an average "subscription" estimate it is impossible to say with any certainty just what the relative distribution volume of these several categories was. Nevertheless, despite these and other obvious limitations on this evidence, the following inferences seem plausible.

First, what might be termed active, functional literacy had expanded well beyond the urban and rural elite to include a very sizeable representation from Mannsaaker's lower strata, including the urban working class.

Secondly, even if we made the patently false assumption that religious issues were limited to periodicals in that category, the expansion of this sector from about 20.7 percent to 28 percent of total output between 1860 and 1900 certainly provides additional evidence for an acceleration of religious interests during this period that is congruent with our earlier descriptions of the timing and tempo of activist mobilization. On the other hand, while it is probable that a disproportionate share of this output was traceable to inner- and outer-mission organizations, it is also probable that this very magnitude reflected the intensity of ideological conflict within and between religious factions. Simply stated, these periodicals *publicized* the dissolution of religious unity *within* that segment of the population most actively concerned with such affairs.

Thirdly, the proliferation of periodicals was generated by both labor force differentiation and more general ideological and intellectual trends.[12] The literate market demand within the primary, secondary, and tertiary sectors of the labor force reflects corresponding changes in relative size and technical interests of the population engaged in such activities. Given our fundamental concern with rural educational achievements, it is of particular significance that while the primary sector declined in employment after 1860, the number of periodicals directed to their interests increased from 3 to 25 between 1860 and 1900.[13] This reverse relationship may be attributed both to technical developments and the increased market orientation (foreign and domestic) of production in farming, fishing, and forestry. On the other hand, the extent to which small land-holders, tenant farmers, and agricultural laborers shared in such reading experiences is, at best, problematic and will concern us later.

Comparative studies in the sociology of literate culture, both elite and popular, as well as general surveys of Norwegian intellectual and social history, point to the probability that the "nonreligious" periodical market was composed disproportionately, if not overwhelmingly, of rural/urban elites in general and professionals in particular. Most obviously, as the number of public and private professionals in law, medicine, education (both mass and elite), etc. increased, publications appealing to their special interests could be sustained and, except for technical legal journals, increased in number. More generally, a clear indicator of market differentiation may be seen in the decline of Tveteraas's "mixed content" category, from 42.5 percent to 28.6 percent of total output during this forty-year period. Publications devoted to special topics, above all to "social questions," constituted a spin-off from that group, as the magnitude of reader interest provided an economic base for their existence. This need not be interpreted as a decline in the audience for general-interest periodicals, but rather as an overall growth of the market.

These few observations provide some sense of that expanding range of published symbolic resources in terms of which alternative life orientations could be articulated as new situations disrupted old expectations. As the number of secular professionals in law, medicine, and education outnumbered the clergy within Norway's professional labor force, something like a secularization of formal normative systems could be diffused from the upper strata to cover larger segments of the population. The proliferation of periodicals devoted primarily to nonreligious issues may be regarded as a rather broadly representative, if only partial, indicator of this process. Contrariwise, the current expansion of religiously oriented periodicals, including their internal ideological cleavages, constituted, at least in part, a published counter-attack in defense of traditional values and normative systems.

Certainly the most thoroughly documented and widely familiar aspect of this dialectic interplay between Lutheran Orthodoxy, both lay and clerical, on the one hand and proponents of Christian and/or secular humanism on the other is to be found in the historiography of Norwegian literature after about 1850. From national romanticism in the 1840s and 1850s to psychological realism in the 1890s, moral–ethical issues and a quest for both national and personal identity pervade the work of Norway's leading men and women of letters. For example, the frequency with which state-church clergymen appear in the works of Ibsen, Bjørnson, Kielland, and others as central characters, usually upholding traditional values in conflict with those being promoted directly or by implication by the author, provides some evidence for the changing social perceptions of the clergy, if only among the urban intelligentsia.[14]

Democratization of clerical recruitment and elite religiosity

The role of successive clerical generations in defining elite religion had been subject to recurrent, though qualified, attack, at least since the spread of rationalism toward the end of the eighteenth century. Challenges, which contracted their religious relevance, expanded downward to include historically visible representations from lower strata, even before 1860, among

Haugeans, Thranaites, diverse sectarians, and early outer- and inner-mission activists. Concurrently, the progressive secularization of advanced educational experiences, together with the clergy's reduction to an ever smaller minority within an expanding professional labor force, continued to erode the relative prestige of clerical careers among its status peers. This rather contradictory combination of challenges to the clergy's spiritual (lower strata) and intellectual (upper strata) qualifications issued in an identity crisis of unprecedented intensity.

These converging role strains must certainly have contributed significantly to the timing and social distribution of the Johnsonian revival. Einar Molland and others have observed that for the first time in Norwegian history a popular religious movement mobilized a sizeable segment of the upper strata. This has been attributed to the fact that its prime carriers were the clergy.[15] Given the sustained rejection of exclusive clerical prerogatives in preaching on the part of lower-strata activists in conflict with these Johnsonian agents, we may infer that their prime audience, at least initially, was composed of status peers.

Theological students, awakened by Professor Johnson, wrote letters home to their families and friends. Summer vacations were increasingly filled with devotional activities at home and at resort centers, which in turn spread an awareness of and commitment to these "new" experiential demands within upper-strata social circles. Their success appears to have been particularly marked in Bergen and, perhaps, West Country cities generally.[16]

Given the instability and vagaries of revival psychology, it is certainly difficult to know just how transitory or permanent such elite experiential commitments proved to be. Most of the evidence, as we shall see, seems to point in the transitory direction, as enthusiasm declined and lower-strata lay activists increasingly dominated the movement's public image.

Twenty-five years after Johnson's appointment to the theological faculty in 1849, his students had all but displaced the previous generation of parish clergymen. It is probable that this process was not regionally random. That is, there were not only rural/urban but considerable regional variations in the desirability of parish appointments. The least attractive positions were concentrated in the economically backward and culturally isolated parishes of northern and western Norway. A newly ordained candidate was most likely to gain his first post in such areas, particularly when, as in the 1850s and 1860s, there was a large over-supply of qualified men seeking employment.[17] When a position fell vacant in the more affluent parishes of eastern and particularly southeastern Norway, the first choice went to already established clergymen with more seniority. If we assume such a directional flow in career mobility,

Table 4.2. *Social-strata origins of the Norwegian clergy, 1801–1910*

Years	I Upper (%)	II Upper-middle (%)	III Lower-middle (%)	IV Lower (%)	Totals (%)
1801–1810	5.5	62.4	27.5	4.6	100.0
1811–1820	9.4	75.5	15.1	—	100.0
1821–1830	8.3	73.3	18.0	0.4	100.0
1831–1840	6.0	61.7	29.9	2.4	100.0
1841–1850	5.2	64.7	28.4	1.7	100.0
1851–1860	11.3	63.7	24.2	0.8	100.0
1861–1870	4.7	54.0	37.6	3.7	100.0
1871–1880	2.5	50.5	45.1	1.9	100.0
1881–1890	3.3	35.7	53.8	7.2	100.0
1891–1900	3.2	40.9	54.8	1.1	100.0
1901–1910	2.7	49.3	46.9	1.3	100.0
Totals 1801–1910	5.1	55.4	37.1	2.4	100.0

Source: Mannsaaker, *Det Norske Presteskapet* (Oslo, 1954), table 23, p. 201, "Prestefedrane fordelte paa ulike samfunnslag." See text for social composition of strata.

then we may infer that Johnsonians displaced their predecessors, on the average, earlier in the west and north and later in the east and southeast.[18]

The implications of this probable displacement pattern will be explored more fully when we return to our consideration of some regional variations in the timing and tempo of mass educational development and lay mobilization after 1860. For the present, any attempt to estimate the impact of Johnsonian clergymen upon elite styles of religiosity must take into account the interplay between this generational shift and what has been called the democratization of the clergy, particularly during the decades after 1860.

Table 4.2 contains Mannsaaker's description of the state-church clergy's social origins during the nineteenth century.[19] What inferences can be made on the basis of this evidence regarding the changing social relations and symbolic content of elite religiosity? Given the relative size of the four indicated strata in the total population, it is evident that those I have labeled an elite (strata I and II) were radically over-represented, even after 1860. This meant, at a minimum, that so far as life-cycle ritual occasions were concerned, they were more often than not relating to men who had experienced similar initial life-situations. Obviously, in the absence of at least three-generational data it is impossible to say just how old or new such shared experiences might have been. It may be suggested, however, that as upward occupational mobility accelerated after about 1860, the proportion of clergymen whose grandfathers had not moved in these higher social circles increased.

Even without such an assumption, the clergy's social declension after 1860 is graphic enough. This is most clearly dramatized if we contrast both the magnitude and historical context of elite representation at the beginning and end of the century. Their presence reached its peak of 85 percent at a time (1811–1820) when the Constitution was written, clergymen were over-represented in the Storting and still constituted a majority group within the professional labor force. Sixty years later, during the politically explosive 1880s, when the clergy were in retreat on all fronts, elite contributions as clerical incubators had been cut to 39 percent of the total. If we accept the generational probabilities suggested above, their effective presence as es-tablished social equals to current elites was even lower.

The turning-point in this process, as in so many others of concern to us, came during the 1860s. Thereafter, recruitment from Mannsaaker's third stratum of lower functionaries, petty bourgeois, and small land-holders, exhibited sustained growth, though still markedly under-represented in proportion to its size. The correspondence between this transition and the Johnsonian displacement was not accidental, although both economic developments and an increase in the absolute number of parish positions was certainly crucial.

Some sense of the "causal mix" here may be gained by contrasting the timing and social composition of a similar downward drift in recruitment to other sectors of the professional labor force. Career opportunities in law, higher education, and medicine, as we have seen, rapidly outnumbered those in theology after 1850. The inevitable expansion in social recruitment, however, was significantly different. Theology attracted students from lower strata earlier, in greater relative numbers, and disproportionately from rural areas. In contrast, the other professions gained such students later, in smaller relative numbers and in greater concentrations from urban areas.[20]

Some of the more plausible and familiar explanations for this contrast would include the greater visibility of clerical role models in rural areas as well as the religious conservatism presumably characteristic of such populations, reinforced in the Norwegian case by sustained Pontoppidan conditioning. Such general considerations can hardly account adequately for the timing of their appearance among the clergy. Briefly, Gisle Johnson's rapid rise to orthodox pre-eminence within the theological faculty, his bitter public attacks against clerical Grundtvigianism in general and Wexels in particular, plus open and active cooperation with latter-day Haugeans and other lay activists encouraged clerical career aspirants among awakened circles of this lower stratum to risk the evils of Oslo.

Whatever the causal mix may have been, the most crucial point to be made here is that the transmission of new and old styles of clerical religiosity was increasingly shaped by upwardly mobile men whose initial life-situations and training experience had, to variable degrees, both isolated them from and heightened their hostility to elite life orientations. The ensuing tensions generated by this process certainly reinforced the growing isolation of elites from effective clerical influence. The progressive social segregation of the Johnsonian clergy from other segments of the *embetsstand* was reflected in and sustained by a significant downward drift in mate selection. We may imagine that earlier patterns of sociability within the *embetsstand* altered somewhat as the proportion of preachers' wives from Mannsaaker's third stratum increased during the latter half of the nineteenth century.[21] Finally, as the official bureaucracy expanded in response to political economic developments, a corresponding specialization of functions issued in a reduction of clerical role tasks, which in turn led to a decline in the frequency of their interaction with other professionals in workday situations.

Certainly Mannsaaker and Aubert were justified in their interpretation of these several interrelated trends as signaling the secularization of at least the urban upper strata. The cleavage between Orthodox Christianity and secular culture, expressed in growing ideological conflicts between Johnsonian activists (both lay and clerical) and the urban intelligentsia, was partially generated by these fundamental systemic changes which were fragmenting the social reconstruction of "realities" in late-nineteenth-century Norwegian society.

What can be said briefly and more directly about the "actual content" of elite styles of religiosity after 1850? There is little or no evidence to indicate that participation in official, life-cycle ritual occasions declined, since this would have entailed formal withdrawal from the state church. It is possible that a disproportionate number of the 5,000 dissenters reported (1891) as outside the church without further religious affiliation were drawn from upper strata.[22] This, in turn, *might* suggest a principled non-participation in such events.

Religious instruction beyond that required for Confirmation continued for at least some of those students who went on to advanced schools, and may have issued in a less parochial and more sophisticated awareness of alternative interpretations of the Christian tradition than was probable for those children whose experience was limited to Pontoppidan. These diversified experiences produced well-educated, if not awakened, Christians. On the other hand, here, as elsewhere in the comparative history of religious commitment, conflicting ideological alternatives probably encouraged detachment, skepticism, and/or indifference with disproportionate frequency. When Gisle Johnson launched his attack on modern disbelief (*vantro*), his most visible point of reference was certainly at these upper levels of the status system. It is, however, important to bear in mind that Johnson's criterion of true religiosity, at best, automatically relegated a vast majority of the population to the status of spiritual somnambulists, however conventional their commitments may have been when measured by earlier definitions.

Just how extensive and sustained Johnsonian modes of ideological/experiential religious expression may have been at this level can be inferred indirectly on the basis of some fragmentary evidence beyond that already cited, most of which points in a negative direction. First, as we have seen and will examine in more detail below, except for the Johnsonian clergy, upper-strata representatives were conspicuous by their relative absence in the Luther Foundation's organizational system between 1868 and 1891. Contrariwise, their presence was probably greater in the less controversial foreign-mission movement.

Secondly, when Einar Molland writes that Lutheran Orthodoxy dominated Norwegian intellectual life until the late 1870s, he qualifies this by saying that "at any rate, Johnsonian theology determined the limits of what scholars and authors could say publicly."[23] His excellent summary of major literary/journalistic trends after 1850 reveals a growing pattern of hostility directed against Johnsonianism in particular and, later, alienation from or indifference to religious traditionalism in general. This became most visible after 1880. It certainly cannot be assumed, however, that the poets, novelists, and dramatists of Norway's literary Golden Age provide wholly reliable and valid indicators of life orientations, religious or otherwise, within Mannsaaker's two upper strata. If more systematic evidence of the changing composition of their most sympathetic readership were assembled, it would probably reveal, as many have assumed, a significant correspondence between the social and regional (e.g., east, urban) distribution of their most receptive audience and the radical, bourgeois left (*rene venstre*).

This is not to say that the secular soul-searching and humanistic presuppositions pervading much of this literature, anathema to Orthodox Johnsonians, failed to strike a responsive chord among politically conservative elites, for many of whom the Johnsonian clergy, if only as social "outsiders," were a kind of negative intellectual reference group. If the clergy's life-cycle ritual prerogatives (including Confirmation) remained acceptable and, perhaps above all, *respectable*, their experiential demands may well have been regarded as vulgar, appropriate to the less cultivated lower strata and, as such, of possible instrumental value in their political struggles with the more overtly secularized left wing of their liberal opposition. Conservative illusions regarding this strategic potential became evident when Johnson and others in the Luther Foundation's executive committee attempted to mobilize their inner-mission affiliates and Bible Messengers in the fight against parliamentarianism. This effort proved to be not only counterproductive but served to dramatize popular perceptions of elite religiosity. Aside from their transparent, self-seeking political motives, it was quickly pointed out in one parish after another that the conservative elite (*høyre*) could hardly be counted among friends of inner-mission objectives. The combination of objective economic exploitation and what was seen as flagrant indulgence in things of the flesh, at least among East Country conservatives, simply enraged the Christian Left (moderate *venstre*). They could easily believe, if not demonstrate, that the condescending indifference of the right counterbalanced the secularism of the left, without providing any of the concrete political economic advantages derived from their uneasy coalition with the latter.[24]

In conclusion, the several indicators of elite religiosity outlined above, from their initial encounters with Pontoppidan, their educational, professional, and social segregation from the Johnsonian clergy and lay activists to the secular content of their internal ideological similarities and differences, certainly provide graphic evidence for a predominantly secularizing profile. Some implications of these trends for mass educational development and popular religious expression will be included in our discussion of that central concern, to which we now return.

5. Mass educational experience and styles of religious expression

Norway's common school teachers were the most immediate and pervasive agents of a formal process whereby old meanings were reaffirmed and new, more secular symbolic resources were introduced to rural, nonelite strata. Their catechistic activities between 1740 and 1840 prepared the groundwork not only for clerical and lay activists but also for other more or less organized agents of symbolic innovation concerned with the practical and ideological exigencies generated by political and economic developments. No clerical generation from the Pietists to the Johnsonians was wholly successful in harnessing this subordinate labor force to its own distinctive ends. On the one hand, the ambulatory system could be seen as a vast if dissolving bulwark of Pontoppidan Confessionalism since his *Explanation* of the Catechism remained in all but universal use as a medium of literacy production until supplemented by other, more worldly materials after 1860. On the other hand, we saw in chapter 2 how cumulative contradictions within this relatively stable (if not stagnant) system contributed to a fundamental cleavage in popular definitions of religiosity and the laicization of spiritual initiative. The Hauge and Inner-Mission movements both embodied this cleavage and provided a supplementary educational context within which reading and public speaking skills could be promoted in the service of their experiential demands.

It is clear from our estimated magnitudes of these and other lay activists circles that they evoked an effective response from a socially and regionally variable minority of the total laity who had undergone the same basic training in Pontoppidan's version of systematic theology. As suggested earlier, the invidious distinction between awakened and, at best, educated Christians was partially anchored in a growing tension between common school universalism and lay movement particularism. This source of tension accelerated after 1860 as the social organization and content of mass literacy production was differentiated at an unprecedented rate. The symbolic impact, religious and otherwise, of this process could hardly have been uniform, given the several regional variations in the timing (early/late) and tempo (slow/rapid) with which it proceeded between 1860 and 1891.

Just what these developmental variations, which preceded the initial high point of Inner-Mission mobilization (1868–1873) by almost a decade, may have contributed to its unevenly distributed success will engage our attention at several points in the following discussion.

The ambulatory system in transition, 1837–1860

The establishment of teacher-training seminaries in each diocese during the 1830s introduced the first really fundamental change in Norway's rural educational labor force since its inception almost a century earlier.[1] Initially, young men of promise were supported in their studies at these new centers. They were expected to return to their home parishes for a period of service, after which they were free to move as more rewarding opportunities became available.

These *seminarister* began to compose a rather self-conscious status group among common school teachers. Their more extensive and diversified training experience carried with it higher levels of official accreditation which opened a wider market for their semiprofessional skills than for an ambulatory teacher or deacon whose training and career were parochial, both in location and content.

The introduction of such outsiders into a parish constituted a potential for some change in the relationships between pastors, teachers, parents, and pupils. A seminarian's inner autonomy was enhanced by the fact that the parish pastor had not been his only teacher or ultimate evaluator, as in the self-contained Confirmation system. As shown in Table 5.1, seminary graduates usually obtained posts as deacons teaching in *fasteskoler* near the main parish church, gradually displacing their homegrown predecessors. Their paraprofessional status was partially defined by the expectation that they would act as pedagogic guides to non-seminarians, ultimately assuming some of the responsibility for teacher training at the local level.

There is contemporary evidence which suggests that these relatively autonomous seminarians were seen as a potential threat to pastoral control over the religious transmission system.[2] As the ministry of church and education began to expand the common school curriculum and initiated the process whereby preparation for Confirmation became only one of several objectives, these specialists, who were among the leaders in implementing the new policies, could begin to feel more like school teachers and less like ambulatory parish catechists. On the other hand, the very label "seminarian" symbolized their continued subordination to church-controlled objectives. It was taken as self-evident that all diocesan seminaries would be directed by the

Table 5.1. *Common school teachers in 1837 and 1853*

	1837		1853	
Type of school	All teachers	Of these, no. of seminarians	All teachers	Of these, no. of seminarians
Rural schools				
Ambulatory	1,826	—	1,996	311
Fixed	198	34	430	275
City schools	118	17	147	92
Total	2,142	51	2,573	678

Source: Dokka, *Fra Allmueskole til Folkeskole* (Oslo, 1967), table 1, p. 48.

pastors of those parishes within which they were located. When, after about thirty years in existence, these combined offices were separated and full-time directors were appointed, they were still staffed by university-trained theologians who could devote their undivided energies to educational affairs.

The extent to which seminarians actually displaced their parochial predecessors by 1853 is shown in Table 5.1. Their relative prominence among fixed school teachers, while a kind of lead indicator of developments after 1860, is overshadowed by the continued dominance of the ambulatory system in rural areas.

Parish catechists to school teachers from farm homes to school houses, 1860–1891

The School Law of 1860 initiated the most fundamental changes since 1740 in the educational experiences of Norway's rural commonality, with far-reaching implications for the processes of symbolic reconstruction of changing social realities. Existentially, the most visible change came as teachers and their pupils moved from scattered farm homes to centrally located school houses. Provincial and diocesan variations in the tempo of this transition are described in Table 5.2 in terms of the changing percentage of school-age children enrolled in the new locations. These figures combine enrollments in two different types of *fasteskoler*. The remarkably high proportion of fixed schools reported as in existence only one year after the new law was enacted can be attributed in large measure to the transitional practice of renting locales until new construction could be completed. Thus, of the

Table 5.2. *Provincial variations in the tempo of educational development as indicated by percentage of pupils attending fixed-school locations in 1861, 1873, and 1891*

	Pupils in new locations						
Diocese and province	1861	1873	1891	Diocese and province	1861	1873	1891
OSLO				**BERGEN**			
Akershus	64	100	100	Hordaland	26	69	92
Østfold	73	100	100	Sogn and Fjordane	44	72	86
Vestfold	56	95	99	Møre and Romsdal	53	79	92
Buskerud	46	87	100				
HAMAR				**TRONDHJEM**			
Hedmark	48	94	100	Sør-Trondelag	54	82	93
Oppland	61	97	100	Nord-Trondelag	61	92	94
AGDER				**TROMSØ**			
Telemark	40	84	98	Nordland	40	67	91
Aust-Agder	47	76	96	Troms	64	80	98
Vest-Agder	29	56	88	Finnmark	74	98	99
Rogaland	28	64	93				

approximately 2,500 such schools reported in 1861, about 2,000 were in rented locations while the remaining 500 buildings, for the most part, had been constructed before the new law came into effect. Generally speaking, such new construction proceeded earlier and more rapidly in Oslo, Hamar, and Trondhjem dioceses and later in Bergen and the two western provinces of Agder diocese, which corresponds to the timing and tempo of fixed-school enrollment in these same areas.[3] By 1890, approximately 3,000 buildings designed with new instructional procedures in mind had been constructed. Another 2,000 or so rented locales provided housing which temporarily met the demands of the new policy. Out of 6,290 rural school districts in 1890, only 968 remained ambulatory.

As Norway's children moved from farm homes to school houses for their education, relationships between pupils, teachers, parents, and pastors were concurrently modified. The establishment of fixed centers in the old ambulatory districts reduced the absolute number of instructional contexts. As this process of consolidation moved forward, the potential for more effective clerical control at the parish level increased.[4] On the other hand, the clergy's *relative* loss of control over teacher training and educational policy, together with other organizational changes, tended to reduce this potential. The introduction of parish school boards, while controlled by the pastor as chairman, qualified his earlier one-man rule. Moreover, specially qualified school inspectors were supposed to be appointed to oversee the new schools as to the pedagogic adequacy of the teachers' performance and the pupils' progress. This incipient separation of pedagogic evaluation from religious functions paralleled that in teacher-training seminaries and marked a further step toward the institutional separation of educational and religious activities.

If the potential for clerical surveillance of the educational process increased in ways qualified above, it obviously declined for parents. Children's tales of the teacher displaced the direct observation of host adults in the ambulatory system. When the parents were left at home, a fundamental break occurred in a pattern which had been sustained for over a century. One of the anticipated consequences of the ambulatory system was that at least a few adults received a kind of continuing education after Confirmation as they listened to the next generation recapitulate its own experience with Pontoppidan.

The transformation of rural school teachers from parish catechists to semi-autonomous paraprofessionals with a potential for collective action as a self-conscious status group was facilitated by the decline of the earlier direct and often humiliating dependence upon their hosts in the ambulatory system. Concurrently, politically determined changes in the mode and amount of remuneration as well as training certification were reflected in a more stabilized educational labor force. Teaching was becoming a significant career option within the rural division of labor. All of these developments enhanced the probability that incipient plausibility structures of more than one variety could emerge in tension with those sustained by clerical and lay activists.

A comparative provincial profile of this process constructed from annual reports to the Ministry of Church and Education initiated in 1861 is provided in Table 5.3. Two years, 1861 and 1873, were selected as adequate for our concern with some quantitative indicators of mass educational resource developments.[5] This twelve-year contrast partly precedes and includes the Luther Foundation's (LF) initial, most intense mobilization period (1868–1873), as described in chapter 3.

Each column in the table conceals ambiguities which will qualify their interpretation. The meaning of column one (percent of teachers *without* certification) is most problematic as an indicator of professionalization, since the paths to and criteria for certification were so diverse, both regionally and over time.[6] The qualifications of those teachers *with* some kind of certification ranged from seminary or the later teacher's "college" graduates to men whose training went only slightly beyond that received by the old ambulatory

Table 5.3. *Educational labor force development (1861–1873), as indicated by teacher certification, length of service, and mode of payment, by province*

Diocese and province	Teachers without certification		Teachers with less than 7 years' service		Teacher salaries in kind	
	1861 (%)	1873 (%)	1861 (%)	1873 (%)	1861 (%)	1873 (%)
OSLO						
Akershus	49	9	46	17	32	18
Østfold	51	10	43	18	33	18
Vestfold	37	12	46	26	24	15
Buskerud	67	21	42	33	27	13
HAMAR						
Hedmark	73	21	37	23	36	17
Oppland	61	28	49	30	40	23
AGDER						
Telemark	33	8	53	45	41	16
Aust-Agder	62	20	54	39	27	19
Vest-Agder	87	35	60	52	45	35
Rogaland	81	27	68	40	42	33
BERGEN						
Hordaland	75	24	55	35	34	18
Sogn and Fjordane	89	14	42	36	39	27
Møre and Romsdal	73	14	47	28	42	24
TRONDHJEM						
Sør-Trondelag	43	14	49	25	31	22
Nord-Trondelag	47	12	38	28	37	21
TROMS						
Nordland	52	9	47	38	29	27
Troms	43	5	60	43	28	24
Finnmark	56	7	64	39	19	7

teachers. Perhaps the safest interpretation of these figures would be to say that they indicate the percentage of rural school teachers *with no more than* an ambulatory training experience.[7]

Column two is least ambiguous and provides a direct indicator of labor force stability which, in turn, can be taken as an indirect indicator of the extent to which teaching had become a career. The diocesan reports on this dimension classify teachers in three categories according to length of service, i.e., those with more than 15 years, 7 to 15, and less than 7 years. I chose the lowest term of service category both for reasons of tabular economy and in order to emphasize the extent to which the high turnover rates characteristic of the ambulatory system were sustained or declined within each province during this twelve-year period. It can be inferred from these figures that in those provinces (e.g., Vest-Agder) where the turnover rate remained high, career stability was lower and the number of ex-school teachers larger than in provinces like Hedmark and Akershus, where the rate was lower. The possible significance of this probability for the provincial variations in the incidence of lay activism, noted in chapter 2, will be examined more closely later.

Column three reports the percentage of teacher incomes paid "in kind" rather than cash. The most significant item within this form of support came in the provision of teachers with rent-free homes to which variable amounts of land were attached, ranging from those with enough land to support two cows to those with none.[8] As we have seen, teaching in the ambulatory system had been a seasonal, part-time activity, payment for which came primarily in the form of food and lodging wherever one happened to be teaching and, to a lesser, very minimal extent, in cash. There is reason to believe that these figures include some continuation of this practice, particularly in Vest-Agder and Rogaland as well as Bergen diocese, declining gradually after the transition to fixed-school locations in these West Country provinces.

These several signs of growth in occupational status-group identity and relative autonomy were reinforced by an increase in the number of teachers per parish clergyman, from 5.7 to 6.7 between 1865 and 1895. The appearance and rather sustained survival of professional periodicals directed to this growing market, while important in themselves, are a further indicator of career stability, incorporation in a money economy, and increased levels of teacher training. By 1891, only 135 out of 3,907 rural teachers were reported as active without advanced training.[9]

Teacher–pupil interaction altered as multiple objectives required different methods of instruction which the new schools and teachers were designed and trained to facilitate. Dokka observes that with specially designed rooms, desks, benches, etc., children could be grouped by age and reading level. Even though the average number of pupils was often larger here than in the previous farm-home settings, more systematic instruction became possible.[10] The earlier catechistic procedure, during which pupils read aloud to each other while the teacher listened, could be so modified that something other than rote memorization of Pontoppidan was more likely to occur.

As the absolute number of school days increased and the relative amount of time devoted to religious instruction declined with the introduction of secular primers and a more differentiated curriculum, teacher–pupil relationships expanded in scope, content, and affective quality as well as (presumably) educational outcome.[11]

Some sense of curricular content before 1860 can be gained by a brief look at some national aggregate figures reporting changes in the percentage of pupils participating in available common school subjects (beyond reading Pontoppidan) by school type between 1837 and 1853. Thus the percentage of ambulatory school children instructed in writing increased during these years from 22 to 40 percent, while some training in arithmetic expanded from 11 to 27 percent. The percentage of fixed-school pupils with such experience in writing increased from 42 to 64 percent and in arithmetic from 33 to 51 percent. Further instruction remained all but nonexistent in the ambulatory system and of minuscule importance for the otherwise more advantaged fixed-school students.[12]

These fundamental changes in the social organization of literacy production were accompanied by the first really massive and effective modifications in the earlier curriculum. It was not simply that religious education became only one aspect of a more differentiated learning experience, but that the very character of the training itself was redefined. An historical orientation displaced the earlier catechistic format as Bible history and/or Bible reading consumed up to and in some areas over half of the time devoted to religious instruction. Moreover, an abbreviated and stylistically simplified edition of Pontoppidan was introduced during the 1860s without lay opposition. As we have seen, the older editions had long been regarded by many teachers as a major block of functional literacy. The linguistic differences between Pontoppidan's Danish text and the several regional vernaculars had been an inhibiting factor which encouraged little more than rote memorization. The traditional catechistic teaching methods which had reinforced this probable outcome were gradually dropped as a less literalistic approach to learning Pontoppidan's essential content became acceptable.[13]

The introduction in 1863 of P. A. Jensen's *Laesebog for Folkeskolen og Folkehjemmet* marked a "secular" beginning of the end of Pontoppidan as an exclusive medium for the production of mass literacy. This *Reading Book for the People in Home and School* differed from Pontoppidan not only in form and content but, most important, in its implicit life orientation. As Hans-Jorgen Dokka writes, it contained "not only technical articles and selections of more general interest, but also anecdotes and rimes, sagas and fairy tales and even items that could call forth a smile or laughter."[14] The adoption of Jensen's reader was compulsory for all rural (but not urban) school districts. During the succeeding "thirteen or fourteen years (*c.* 1863–1877), 250,000 copies were printed and distributed around the country to schools and homes."[15]

Dokka traces the opposition to this radical curricular innovation to both "contextual" and ideological sources. Pontoppidan had been taught at *a* home under *a* parent's surveillance. Jensen's worldy collection was being introduced at precisely the same time that such direct observation was disappearing at a rapid pace. Widespread protests came from two directions, both of which were against readings from popular and fine literature. The most well-organized and effective opposition came from lay activists who regarded these selections as irreconcilable with Christian faith and morals. Some of these same items were objected to by nonactivists as simply impractical and not leading to that "objective and sober orientation which the times demanded."[16] Secular knowledge of clear instrumental value had never been significantly opposed as such by the rural laity, awakened or otherwise. Hans Nielsen Hauge, for example, was well known to have been a preeminently practical man and had enjoyed the occasional reading of technically useful works.

Unlike the Pontoppidan controversy of the 1840s, popular opposition to Jensen proved only partially successful, as in the elimination of some of the more objectionable items from later editions. These secular inroads were irreversible, as demographic, political, and economic development progressively demanded new knowledge and skills, the inculcation of which gradually reduced the relative amount of time devoted to religious education during the days and weeks of an expanding school year.[17]

The experiential impact of all these educational developments was not randomly distributed socially or regionally. It was differentiated along lines of stratification and cross-cutting regional contrasts, to which we will now turn our attention more directly.

The rural proletariat's educational experience and styles of religious expression, 1860–1891

The relative size and internal composition of Mannsaaker's third and fourth strata altered significantly during the nineteenth century and particularly after about 1850. Internal migration contributed to the growth of Norway's urban

Table 5.4. *Aggregate migration from Norway for selected periods, 1836–1900*

Years	No. of outmigrants	Years	No. of outmigrants
1836–1845	6,200	1866–1875	119,545
1846–1855	32,270	1876–1890	226,932
1856–1865	39,350	1891–1900	94,854

Source: Norges Officielle Statistikk, VII, no. 25, *Utvandringsstatistikk*, 1921, section V, pp. 26–35

population between 1845 and 1891 from 12.2 to 23.7 percent of the national population (1,328,471 and 2,000,917 for the earlier and later year respectively). An official report from the year 1876 recorded almost 60,000 persons living in dioceses other than those in which they were born. An additional 37,260 residents were born outside the country.[18] Both of these were within a national aggregate population of about 1,813,424.

Obviously, the most dramatic demographic phenomenon during this period was the massive migration to America. Table 5.4 provides some sense of the timing, tempo, and magnitude of this movement.

Tenant farmers, agricultural day laborers, and servants composing our fourth stratum constituted a disproportionate number of both internal and external migrants. The former expanded the urban proletariat while both contracted the relative size of the rural proletariat. All this facilitated a partial reversal of stratification trends which characterized several decades *before* 1850, summarized by Semmingsen in this way:

A comparatively high proportion of the increase in population (*c.* 1800–1855) had to be satisfied with a place in the lower social strata of the society. If any social mobility could be found in the agricultural society of this period, it would in any event be in part a movement with a downward trend. The proletariat of agricultural workers continued to increase, particularly in those parts of the country where the farms were big and needed much hired labour. The social distance between farmer and labourer increased, and a growing social tension developed inside the agricultural society. This tension exploded briefly but with intensity in the workers' movement under Marcus Thrane's leadership in 1849–51.[19]

Estimating the relative size of Mannsaaker's two lower strata remains problematic in view of the noncomparability of the census categories utilized between 1801 and 1891 in describing the occupational composition of the national population in both rural and urban areas. Nevertheless, two general statements seem justified by the evidence. First, these two strata, composing the "commoners" in contrast to the "cultured elite," constituted something

Table 5.5. *Estimates of rural labor force dependency, 1801–1845*

Year	Independent	Dependent
1801	83,000	203,000
1825	90,000	212,000
1835	103,000	225,000
1845	105,000	245,000

Source: Steen, *Det Gamle Samfunn*, pp. 55–59 *et passim*

over 90 percent of the total population. Second, the fourth stratum probably outnumbered the third by about 2 to 1 during most of the nineteenth century, reaching its highest *rural* imbalance about 1850. It declined thereafter as emigration and urbanization contracted the relative size of the rural proletariat. Tenant farmers, composing only one element within that stratum, declined from 26 percent of the rural population in 1845 to 4.2 percent in 1910.[20]

Professor Steen provides a persuasive quantitative description and analysis of rural strata *before* 1850 which may be condensed and conceptually translated into our categories as follows: (1) our third stratum corresponds to part of what I will term Steen's "independent" stratum of land owners, although his includes both estate and large land owners; (2) our fourth stratum corresponds to what may be labeled Steen's "dependent" population, composed of tenant farmers with or without land, day laborers, and servants. Given these qualifications, the summary estimates in Table 5.5, adapted from Steen, may be suggested.[21] Some idea of the ambiguities hidden within such crude figures may be gained from a brief look at some census data from the years 1876 and 1891 which can also serve as partial indicators of rural stratification trends after 1845. First, a table in the 1876 report provides a description of the male population over fifteen years of age in rural areas according to whether a given life-situation (*livsstillinger*) was the sole, the chief, or a secondary source of livelihood. The national aggregate items in Table 5.6 are extracted and adapted from that source.[22]

The census table from which the data in Table 5.6 were selected did not include tenant farmers without land, agricultural laborers, servants, women, or children below fifteen years of age, and hence radically understates the relative size of the dependent population during this year. The purpose of its

Table 5.6. *Occupational combinations in the rural labor force, 1876*

Occupation	Source of livelihood			
	Sole	Chief	Secondary	Totals
Farmer	78,876	26,080	21,142	126,098
Tenant farmer	30,185	17,713	6,256	54,154
Fisherman	17,725	10,012	23,066	50,803
Total	126,786	53,805	50,464	

inclusion here, however, was to provide some perspective on the rather mixed internal composition of these "occupational" strata – a phenomenon the relevance of which will be touched upon later.

Finally, the rural labor force statistics for 1891, which include *both* males and females over the age of fifteen, report:[23]

1 121,234 farm owners (Independent)
2   33,110 tenant farmers, with and without land (Dependent)
3   84,190 "hired servants" including agricultural day laborers, household help, etc. (Dependent)
4   71,121 "kin group servants" (Status Ambiguous)

Just how the persons within this last category should be distributed between "Independent" and "Dependent" within the larger societal class hierarchy is uncertain. They (apparently) consisted of relatives and of children over fifteen years of age still living at home. It seems probable that well over half of these could be assigned to the "Independent" farm-owner category, since it was highly probable that the children of tenant farmers and others lower in the status hierarchy would leave home as servants or laborers, often even before the age of fifteen. A conservative estimate of 50 percent each way would issue in a rural labor force in 1891 of about 157,000 Independent and 153,000 Dependent persons in such life-situations. Obviously, so far as Mannsaaker's fourth stratum is concerned, this leaves out of account the expanding urban proletariat. Given our principled neglect of urban mass educational developments due to data difficulties, the discussion to which we now turn will, as in chapter 2, be limited largely to some aspects of the educational experience and styles of religious expression of rural populations, with occasional reference to some urban evidence.

The educational opportunities and experiences of the rural proletariat continued to vary regionally and over time. To repeat, while they shared in the universal encounter with Pontoppidan, the frequency and the social context within which it occurred must have colored their experience in significant ways. The number of school days available to them within the ambulatory system had been both objectively lower and subjectively less accessible than it was for the children of socially superior freeholders to whose homes they often walked for instruction.

This contrast, as we have seen, was most sharply drawn in eastern Norway. There were fundamental regional differences in both farm-community organization and the social linkages of the dependent labor force. Farm units from South Trondelag to Østfold were not only larger but tended to be spatially dispersed in both the valleys and the highland meadows. West Country holdings, while often smaller and less productive than even some tenant farms in the east, were frequently organized in cooperative clusters along the fjords and in the mountain meadows where collective efforts prevailed.

According to Freimannslund, western "cottagers were often close relatives of the farmer and his family, and the permanent servants originated largely from other peasant families in the same parish." She also asserts that "in the south-eastern regions and in Trondelag, social divisions between the farmer and his farm-hands were more marked. In more recent times the cottagers and servants often came from other parishes, the servants came from cottages and were only rarely farmer's sons and daughters."[24] Given such contextual contrasts, we may imagine that Pontoppidan's questions and answers bearing on the Fourth Commandment and enjoining love and obedience to all those whom God had set over them, explicitly including landlords and employers, were memorized with an edge of bitterness or resentment in the east less likely to prevail in the west. The reciprocal catechistic obligations of paternalistic social superiors regarding their subordinates were clearly more vulnerable to market fluctuations and the calculations of contract in the east.[25] A fundamental issue in the Thrane movement was generated precisely over these relationships, or, more correctly, their imminent collapse under pressure of explosive population growth which, as seen above, could not be absorbed in the established order.

The probability that any popular movement, religious or otherwise, could recruit a following evenly distributed across class lines under such conditions was certainly minimal. The relative insignificance of evangelical themes to the content of social protest expressed by this East Country stratum seems particularly evident when we remember that Marcus Thrane mobilized some 20,000 to 30,000 tenant farmers and agricultural and urban workers primarily from eastern provinces in *three* years, while the national Inner-Mission required some *forty* years to reach a membership of 28,000 throughout all of Norway.[26] As the urban segment of this stratum increased between 1865 and 1891, there is little or no reason to believe that the experiential criteria of Johnsonian/Inner-Mission religiosity became any more salient or relevant to the redefinition of their life-situations than it had been earlier.

East Country rural proletarians shared in the early and rapid transition from farm homes to school houses which distinguished Oslo and Hamar from Bergen and southwestern Agder dioceses. Concurrently, the curriculum differentiated more rapidly, and the proportion of career teachers as measured by tenure, training, and cash remuneration was greatest here. The fact that amplified symbolic resources of a more secular character became available *before* Gisle Johnson's students were promoted from their career beginnings in the north, west, or south to the more affluent east-southeastern parishes, *combined with* built-in status barriers, certainly helped to reduce receptivity to evangelical options still further.

Contrariwise, in the west and southwestern parishes, lay mobilization, combined with earlier Johnsonian clerical appointments, *preceded* these same educational developments, which moved forward much more gradually. It may be suggested that this facilitated the incorporation of new symbolic resources within a more established religious rhetoric in the relative absence of class conflicts generating alternative ideological requirements. If West Country anticlericalism often seemed more intransigent at times, it may be attributed in part to more pronounced core/periphery hostilities in which the clergy remained the major representative of the former. In the relative absence of other status distinctions, their hostility could be directed against such outsiders in a more single-minded fashion. Easterners had a wider range of status targets to resent.[27]

Pastors, teachers, and lay preachers provided a disproportionate share of this rural stratum's formal contact with the larger world. Unlike the three higher strata, however, they did not include the presence of status equals among those agents of symbolic continuity and change in anything approximating a proportionate number. The 2.4 percent of the clergy that rose from that life-situation between 1801 and 1910, with the interesting and possibly significant exception of the decade 1881–1891, all but eliminates this source of informal influence.

Direct evidence regarding the social origins of school teachers is limited to studies of students enrolled in diocesan seminaries and, later, other teacher-training centers. Semmingsen writes that a study of the school statistics from the years 1875–90 shows that more than 95 % of the students of the training colleges came from rural districts; a little over two-thirds of the students were sons of farmers; rather more than one-tenth were sons of crofters [tenant farmers] and other agricultural labourers; the rest were themselves sons of elementary-school teachers or came from other strata of society. Statistics covering the place of domicile of the pupils are lacking but indirect evidence suggests that the western part of the country was strongly represented among the students of the training colleges.[28]

Helge Dahl, in his comparison of student origins at the older diocesan seminaries and the provincial teacher schools established during the 1860s, observes that while they came from essentially the same strata, the new schools, relatively speaking, recruited a significantly higher proportion from the homes of tenant farmers. Nevertheless, with some notable exceptions (e.g., Nesset and Rakkestad parishes), these students were drawn largely from the lower levels of Mannsaaker's third stratum.[29]

Finally, as we shall see shortly, in so far as the occupational labels which Rudvin reports for the Luther Foundation's Bible Messengers can be taken as representative for lay preachers in general, we would have to conclude that an even smaller percentage of preachers than teachers was drawn from this lowest stratum. Given the limited control tenants and servants had over their work-time patterns, this is hardly surprising in view of the demands placed upon Bible Messengers.

Pastors, teachers, and lay preachers within lower-middle strata

It seems probable that Mannsaaker's highly heterogeneous lower-middle stratum of small land-owners, petty bourgeois, and lower official func-tionaries experienced a higher level of status ambiguity more frequently than most individuals located in those strata above or below them in the hierarchy. Meagre incomes from small holdings in the East Country were commonly supplemented by work for larger farmers and/or owners of timber tracts as seasonal forestry workers. This variable blend of economic autonomy and dependence made for a social marginality which blurred status distinctions *vis-à-vis* landless agricultural workers, servants, and tenant farmers. Such marginality was sharply reduced in the West Country, where the social organization of production in small-scale agriculture and fishing enterprise sustained egalitarian attitudes. Work situations required the intimate cooper-ation of both employers and employees, whatever the distribution of ownership may have been. Moreover, as we have seen, they were often either related or at least from the same parish.

These broad regional contrasts were crosscut by nationwide opportunities for at least part-time employment as teachers, deacons, or bailiffs – positions which comprised most of those "lower official functionaries" in Mannsaaker's third stratum. Still other occupational combinations prevailed at this level, but these must suffice to establish its *relatively* distinctive profile in partial contrast with the strata immediately above and below it. This contrast, of course, was not absolute but a matter of relative proportion as between strata, since combined economic interests and activities were to be found within all of them.

Once again, the educational developments which have concerned us thus far were experienced most directly and effectively by children from this stratum. Unlike children from higher strata, their encounter with Pontoppidan was less likely to be diluted or contradicted by alternative symbolic resources gained from a more differentiated educational experience or informally absorbed as part of a life style. Moreover, if it is true that teacher–pupil status proximity facilitates the learning process and, contrariwise, status distance inhibits it, then the fact that such discrepancies were smallest for children from this stratum lends additional weight to our argument that the impact of parish school changes after 1860 were most sustained and effective at this level. Given the variations in size of landholdings within this stratum, there may have been corresponding differences in the intensity of educational experience similar to but not as great as those between strata.

As pupils and teachers moved from farm homes to school houses, a process of consolidation occurred which, in a sense, rationalized the relationship between parish pastors and their educational labor force. Concurrently, the social origins of that clergy (see Table 4.2) moved down and somewhat closer to that of their teachers. Above all, farmers' sons began to pursue clerical careers for the first time in significant numbers. During the period between 1801 and 1860, 58 men derived from that context, about evenly divided between the homes of large farmers (29 from stratum II) and small farmers (27 from stratum III). Between 1861 and 1880 farmer recruitment escalated to 83, and their social origins altered radically with 67 and 16 drawn from small and large farm settings respectively. This downward drift continued during the next twenty years (1881–1900), as only 9 out of 111 farm-generated clergyman stemmed from Mannsaaker's second stratum, which included large landholders.[30]

The regional distribution of this rural recruitment pattern shifted from the East Country dioceses to those of the south and west (Agder, Bergen), most notably after 1861.[31] In so far as comparable trends characterized geographic recruitment at teacher-training centers (as Semmingsen suggests), we may infer that where such men worked together in the same parish, earlier status distinctions were less salient. Moreover, given the probability that these men were more likely to be receptive to, if not always actually agents of, the Johnsonian/Inner-Mission movement than either urban or East Country candidates, we may infer that their growing presence within the religious/educational role system would facilitate the diffusion of experiential styles of religious expression, even into otherwise resistant eastern parishes.

Given the rather wide intra-stratum (III) variations in farm size, productivity, and income, it seems highly probable that Mannsaaker's small-farm theological students came from the upper end of that distribution, as some of the problems he encountered in distinguishing between candidates from large and small farms suggests. More obviously, the hard cash needed to finance formal educational experience beyond the parish school level was unlikely to be generated by those small farmers whose meagre holdings forced supplementary employment in order to make ends meet. Teacher training was obviously much less expensive, both because of the relative absence of secondary school prerequisites and because such schools were distributed throughout each diocese and province. Finally, after 1860 the sons of rural school teachers begin to appear with an accelerating and disproportionate frequency among the parish clergy, which points to an inter-generational occupational mobility pattern familiar not only in Norway but elsewhere. That is, the homes of rural (and urban?) school teachers became ever more conspicuous as incubators for the next step up in professional advancement.[32] The grandson of a marginal small land-holder might become an ordained parish clergyman via a school-teacher parent.

I have argued repeatedly that lay mobilization from Haugeans to Inner-Mission activists and adherents was disproportionately centered in this stratum. Much of the evidence for this assertion is indirectly based on certain expectations about the interplay between mobile middle-strata life situations and styles of religious expression derived from the sociological literature on post-Reformation popular religiosity. Late nineteenth-century elites and proletarians, with some regional qualifications, were (at best) more likely to be found among those spiritual somnambulists, educated rather than awakened Christians, who constituted an evangelistic challenge to inner-mission lay preachers as well as the Johnsonian clergy.[33]

More direct evidence for these assertions has been based on a comparison of the changing social composition and career patterns of the state-church clergy and, less reliably, parish school teachers. Broadly representative evidence required for the construction of such a comparative profile is obviously most accessible here, since both were public servants whose positions were a matter of official concern, support, and record-keeping. A comparable profile of nineteenth-century lay preachers obviously poses a stickier set of historiographic problems. The major and most reliable sources derive from primary research on the Hauge and Inner-Mission movements.[34]

Ola Rudvin, in an appendix to his account of LF's activities between 1868 and 1891, provides short biographical sketches of almost 220 Bible Messengers (*Bibelbud*) and emissaries who were in LF's service for variable time periods during that initial stage of mobilization. This, to my knowledge, constitutes the only systematic though incomplete inventory of something like lay preachers available in the current literature. It should be noted immediately that these men probably represented a minority of all lay preachers active at that time. As we have seen, regional associations and some local societies, particularly those not affiliated with LF, engaged their own men who were uninhibited by LF's equivocal Emergency Principle. Just what, if any, systematic difference there may have been in the occupational backgrounds of these two groups of lay activists can only be a matter of conjecture. There were, particularly during the 1840s and 1870s free-lance lay preachers whom neither the Haugeans nor the Inner-Mission managed to control except by excluding them from their own circles and warning others against them. Just how numerous these men were or what their social provenance was remains an open question, unless we include the agents of dissenter groups with their greater historical visibility in that category.[35]

Table 5.7, distilled from Rudvin's sketches,[36] provides a summary profile of LF's Bible Messengers active between 1868 and 1891, cross-classified by diocese and province of origin and according to their primary, full-time occupational label or labels. Each column requires some clarification before a few interpretive commentaries are made. The least ambiguous category is that composed of teachers, deacons, and a small number of theological candidates. A closer examination of the career patterns of the last group reveals the following. Several had been *seminarister*, teachers, lay preachers, and/or emissaries for LF or Inner-Mission locals before assuming regular parish posts or other types of pastoral activity. It can only be suggested, not demonstrated, that a majority of them were among that growing proportion of clerical candidates recruited from our lower-middle stratum. Professor Johnson's doctrinal purity, as we have seen, had encouraged young men (and their parents) from activist circles to pursue clerical careers which had hitherto been ideologically suspect.

Column four contains 46 men of diverse, often combined occupations, several of whom might have been placed in column one. Of the total included

Table 5.7. *Regular occupations of Luther Foundation Bible Messengers, 1868–1891, by diocese and province of birthplace*

Diocese and province	Teachers deacons, theolog. students	Farmers	Craftsmen and merchants	Combined and miscellaneous	Total
OSLO (totals)	10	11	10	18	49
Akershus	—	4	5	8	17
Østfold	4	3	2	1	10
Vestfold	2	—	2	2	6
Buskerud	4	4	1	7	16
HAMAR (totals)	7	9	2	5	23
Hedmark	2	3	1	2	8
Oppland	5	6	1	3	15
AGDER (totals)	18	15	11	11	55
Telemark	6	1	2	2	11
Aust-Agder	3	—	—	4	7
Vest-Agder	5	8	3	3	19
Rogaland	4	6	6	2	18
BERGEN (totals)	16	15	6	4	41
Hordaland	2	3	4	2	11
Sogn and Fjordane	9	6	1	—	16
Møre and Romsdal	5	6	1	2	14
TRONDHJEM (totals)	9	4	2	1	16
Sør-Trondelag	5	2	—	1	8
Nord-Trondelag	4	2	2	—	8
TROMSØ (totals)	6	2	2	7	17
Nordland	4	1	—	1	6
Troms	2	1	2	6	11
Finnmark	—	—	—	—	—
Totals	66	56	33	46	201

here, 18 reported occupations of a religious and/or educational nature, often combined with agricultural, craft, or mercantile activities. Emissaries, colporteurs, and lay preachers were most prominent among these.

Column two, while superficially the most homogeneous, obscures socio-economic differences of unreported variability. Rudvin's term, *gaardbruker*, while normally not used with reference to tenant farmers (*husmann*) or agricultural laborers, could be applied to a wide range of land-owners. It seems probable, however, that if any of them had been large farmers by Mannsaaker's criteria, this would have been sufficiently unusual to be noted in their short biographical sketches.

The 33 individuals classified in column three as merchants or craftsmen includes 7 shoemakers and 7 carpenters, occupations at least anecdotally familiar elsewhere in Protestant Europe among lay activists within lower-middle strata. Relative to the other three categories, a disproportionate number of men in this group were born and/or worked in urban areas.

These men were screened either directly or indirectly by LF's central steering committee, the members of which lived in or near Oslo. It is not, perhaps, necessary to repeat that this introduced a selective bias in favor of the most accommodating and against the more militant laymen, and thereby qualified the validity of these data as indicators of the larger inner-mission population.

The social composition of the committee itself is relevant here.[37] A total of 38 men had served for varying time periods between 1868 and 1891 on this 12-member committee. Of these almost half (18) were or had been either parish pastors (14), theological faculty professors (2), or engaged in directly related activities. The remainder include men classifiable as merchants and/or in the craft industry (9), professionals (5), and middle-level functionaries in public or private employment (4). Rudvin's sketches are seldom detailed enough to eliminate all ambiguity regarding their relative social standing. Nevertheless, it seems justifiable to assert on the basis of these sketches, scattered references, and logical inference from the text, that committee members were recruited disproportionately from our second stratum and the higher levels of that just below. If three-generational data were to be obtained for these men this issue could be clarified. Given the hostility expressed by the Oslo clerical hierarchy when they initiated their coordination activities in 1868, it is perhaps plausible to infer that at best a minority (e.g., Professor Johnson) of these men derived from established life-situations in the first or second stratum.

When Rudvin asserts that LF and the Inner-Mission Movement more generally recruited a following from all social strata, our evidence would suggest that this was at best representational and not proportional to the relative size of these strata in the national population. Certainly, as claimed earlier, most evidence points to a dramatic under-representation from Mannsaaker's fourth stratum of tenant farmers and agricultural and urban workers. On the other hand, given our continuing uncertainty regarding the relative size of the top two strata, a more cautious, tentative position on these proportional questions seems called for. As I tried to indicate in chapter 4 styles of religious expression at these levels was much more likely to be of a conventional life-cycle ritual and/or humanistic secular variety than one congruent with the more experiential criteria of religiosity prevailing among Inner-Mission activists. We will return to these and related issues in the final chapter after a short comparative case study of the interplay between educational and religious change within two selected provinces.

Hedmark and Vest-Agder: a comparative profile

Our regional contrasts thus far have been limited to east/west generalities and/or a few more refined indicators of variations within dioceses and between provinces. The late Stein Rokkan and his associates at Bergen in their construction of an ever more exhaustive Norwegian historical ecological data archive have frequently been able to utilize the commune (*herred*) as their basic descriptive unit and thereby overcome some of the distortions inherent in larger reporting areas. Their thoroughgoing analyses of regional variations in voting behavior since about 1882, when the first most useful partisan electoral statistics became available, has been sustained for over twenty years. As the almost archaeological reconstructions in chapter 3 make evident, no such *official* description of voluntary religious activism exists except for the very small dissenter population.[38] Nevertheless, an appreciation of a few subprovincial variations may be gained from a brief examination of two "extreme" cases: Vest-Agder and Hedmark.

If it were possible to rank Norway's eighteen provinces along Glock and Stark's five-dimensional scale of religiosity based on historical evidence since the late eighteenth century, I would anticipate that Vest-Agder would be at or near the top, and Hedmark, if not at the bottom, would be very close to it. Secondly, except for the pupil/teacher ratios, these two provinces are at or near the opposite ends of our educational development index for the period between 1860 and 1891. Finally, if we accept differential distributions of power, prestige, and privilege as the single most crucial set of contextual variables, then Vest-Agder constitutes a marked egalitarian extreme even for the West Country. Contrariwise, Hedmark, while not as distinctive in the opposite direction, may still be taken as representative of the socially polarized East Country, with abundant evidence of intense class conflict, cleavages, and consciousness within its population.[39]

Evidence to support the ranking of these two provinces at the opposite ends of a religiosity scale can be first reviewed and then extended. As we have seen, Vest-Agder had been the major rural exception to Herrnhut Pietism's urban concentration after 1770. Hans Nielsen Hauge, during his travels between 1798 and 1804, had found the coastal parishes between Kristiansand and Stavanger more receptive to his message than any other single region. When the Norwegian Mission Society was founded in Stavanger (1842), its locals were concentrated here and only later spread significantly to other rural areas of Norway. Further, in so far as factionalism reflects greater religious concern, the appearance and maintenance of the first anti-Haugean splinter group near here after 1825 are consistent with our other evidence.

Finally, Eilert Sundt, in his remarkable work, *Om Saedelighedstilstanden i Norge (On Moral Conditions in Norway*; first edition, 1857), provides what many contemporary sociologists of religion would accept as a reasonably valid indicator of "consequential religiosity." Using vital statistics for the years between 1830 and 1850, he was able to rank Norway's 53 deaneries in terms of the number of illegitimate births for every 100 legitimate marriages.[40] Lister deanery, the center of late eighteenth-century Pietism in Vest-Agder, sustained its number one position as the unit with the lowest number of births out of wedlock throughout this twenty-year period. Mandal, the other deanery composing Vest-Agder province (then known as Lister og Mandal Ampt.), moved from a rank of two to three.

Hedmark province, on the other hand, was composed of all or parts of three deaneries which ranked close to the opposite end of this scale of "moral conditions" as defined by Sundt, i.e., Hedemarken (forty-fifth), parts of Øvre Romerike (forty-seventh) and Østerdalen (forty-ninth). Pietist influence in Hedmark appears to have been nil. The Haugean impact was weaker here than in any province south of Troms to the far north. Hauge reports having visited some of the parishes (e.g., Grue) from Elverum south to the Akershus/Østfold border, and it was precisely in this more accessible region that the first Inner-Mission Societies (or at least LF affiliates) were established. In addition to our consequential indicator, perhaps the most persuasive evidence regarding religious orientations in Hedmark before 1868 is also indirect and negative. Edvard Bull estimates that two-thirds of the 30,000 persons mobilized in the Thrane movement came from this province.[41] Moreover, it has sustained this pattern of political economic radicalism, as demonstrated by Rokkan's studies of regional variations in voting behavior, from 1882 to the present.[42] It is perhaps justifiable to summarize these few provincial contrasts by citing popular stereotypes current one hundred years later. That is, if Vest-Agder remained in the Bible Belt (*svarte kysten*), Hedmark came to be known as the "red province" by virtue of its massive socialist/communist voting patterns just after the Second World War.

Given these marked historical differences in orientations to things temporal and eternal, it is rather surprising that by 1891 Hedmark's share of LF's affiliates was slightly more than proportional to its part of the national population. This puzzlement may be reduced but not eliminated by a closer scrutiny and interpretation of some additional evidence which will sharpen the contrast between these two provinces.

First, by 1876 all but four of Vest-Agder's twenty parishes reported locals affiliated with LF. Given 36 societies in sixteen parishes, it is obvious that several multilocal parishes existed. It is likely that even these figures constitute an underestimation, since locals unwilling to compromise with the Emergency Principle may have been present in unknown numbers. Two of the four parishes not listed by Rudvin (Siridal, Aaseral) are located in the interior, not near the coast.

Ten of Hedmark's twenty-five parishes are absent from the list of local affiliates in the same year.[43] It is significant, however, that of the fifteen reported as containing such activity, six represented "two-parish" locals, i.e., Hamar-Vang, Kongsvinger-Vinger, and Romedal-Stang. The first two included the only officially defined towns in the province with their surrounding communes. The inference seems clear that mobilization at this stage was too low to sustain separate societies in each area. Six of the ten parishes not reporting affiliates were located in Upper Østerdalen. Unlike the four parishes in up-country Vest-Agder, their absence cannot be attributed so much to isolation, since the Oslo-to-Trondhjem railroad which traversed Hedmark from south to north was nearing completion (1877) at precisely this same time. The construction workers engaged in this enterprise were recruited from both within and without the region and were given rather special attention by LF emmisaries and others. Furthermore, three out of the fifteen assemblies of laymen held between 1856 and 1860 and described by Rudvin as partially preparing the way for LF were located in Hedmark province: one in Hamar, the provincial capital (1856) and two at Tynset far up in Østerdalen (1857, 1859).[44]

We may reasonably conclude from this that Hedmark had experienced something close to its share of evangelistic attention. The most crucial question here relates to the extent to which such efforts were initiated and/or sustained from within Hedmark and not by agents (including the clergy) sent in from outside the province. The basic local history research required to answer this question has not, to my knowledge, been done. Nevertheless, some additional inferences may be drawn from evidence beyond that already cited.

Agder diocese reported eight subprovincial associations of parish locals by 1873, while Hamar contained none until 1886. Four of the former – Kristiansand, Farsund, Flekkefjord, and Mandal associations – were organized within Vest-Agder, which probably reflects its greater organizational maturity based on foreign-mission foundations. Given Hedmark's larger and more dispersed population, its low and late organizational growth rate may be interpreted as a reflection of a very small audience demand for the coordination of evangelistic efforts, in sharp contrast with evangelistic market conditions in Vest-Agder.

Finally, provincial variations in the origins and occupational composition of LF's Bible Messengers provides some additional clues when examined more closely. Our data not only exclude the most militant lay activists but also distort the probable magnitude of provincial differences in the production of lay preachers in other ways. For example, given the sharp contrast in organizational expansion, both horizontally (locals) and vertically (associations), between Hedmark and Vest-Agder, it is highly probable that our data are more representative of the larger situation in Hedmark than in Vest-Agder. That is, if the latter's four subprovincial associations also sponsored lay preachers not included in our table, it follows that the actual level of lay preacher productivity in Vest-Agder was under-represented. Granted this plausible inference, we may conclude that on a hypothetical scale of lay preacher productivity as an additional religiosity indicator, these two provinces, once again, would be even farther removed from each other than the evidence presented already indicates.

The differences in proportional representation from each of the four occupational categories among the men from these two provinces, on first examination, is not so notable. That is, about 25 percent of the total in each province were recruited from among teachers, and about 40 percent engaged in farming as their regular pursuit. Hedmark was over- and Vest-Agder was under-represented in our last two groups in table 5.7, i.e., craftsmen and merchants, combined and miscellaneous. A closer consideration suggests the following tentative interpretations, bearing in mind that the numbers are too small to justify very firm assertions.

Primary-sector occupations (e.g., farming) were obviously far and away the most under-represented of all among those engaged in by LF's Bible Messengers, with only about 26 percent of the total recruited from this sector. The degree to which this under-representation occurred varied from one province to another, depending on its occupational structure, which in turn varied with the degree of urbanization. The proportions reported as coming from the primary sector in Hedmark were 3 out of 8 and in Vest-Agder 8 out of 19. These are greater than the national aggregate proportional figure. Their similar magnitude suggests the following interpretation. Hedmark was far above the national average in the proportion of its population engaged in the primary sector, i.e., farming and forestry. As late as 1891, only 5,480 persons resided in "urban" areas (Hamar, Kongsvinger) while 113,649 remained rural. Vest-Agder, according to the same census, reported a population distribution of 19,833 in urban and 58,905 in rural areas. Their similar "farmer/Bible Messenger" proportions, in light of these contrasts, point to radical differences in the extent to which their respective rural populations were penetrated by religious activism. That is to say, on a hypothetical "degree-of-penetration" scale, Hedmark and Vest-Agder, once again, would be located at the extremes of low and high penetration respectively.

The timing and tempo of educational development in these two provinces reveal differences of comparable magnitude. Vest-Agder's rural schools preserved attributes characteristic of the ambulatory system longer than any other single province. Its relative standing on our index was particularly pronounced by 1873, when the developmental gap between it and the provinces nearest to it in "retarded growth" was widest. Its closest competitor for this bottom position on two of the four indicators was the neighboring province of Rogaland, which also rivaled its high religiosity score as measured by organizational criteria.

Hedmark's relative standing is less consistent. Perhaps the most reliable, valid and "revealing" of these indicators is that showing the percentage of pupils enrolled in fixed schools. By 1873, 94 percent of Hedmark's children had made the move from farm homes to schoolhouses, whether rented or specially constructed, in contrast to 56 percent of Vest-Agder's school-age population. By this measure Hedmark is clearly among those provinces in which the ambulatory system was displaced most rapidly.

Hedmark's educational labor force appears to have been the most stable and experienced in Norway, as indicated by the percentage of teachers with less than seven years' service. By 1873, it was surpassed on this dimension only by Akershus and Østfold. Vest-Agder and Rogaland, on the other hand, rather consistently generated the largest number of ex-school teachers, as indicated by the very high percentage of those with less than seven years' service. This contrast in the extent to which teaching had become a career is sustained when comparing the relative proportion of teachers in the two provinces with more than fifteen years of service. The percentage in this category increased from 34 to 42 percent in Hedmark and 17 to 20 in Vest-Agder between 1861 and 1873.

Further, variations in the extent to which educational services were remunerated in kind rather than cash, as well as the decline in that mode of support between 1861 and 1873, are rather broadly congruent with other indicators of educational development. Once again, Vest-Agder and Rogaland are sharply distinguished from the other provinces by their high and continued reliance on non-monetary modes of remuneration, a distinction which became even more pronounced by 1873. Meanwhile, the percentage of teachers' payment in Hedmark in this category dropped from 35 to 17 percent, which was one of the three lowest in Norway (outside of Finnmark).

All this seems rather clear at the provincial level (in rural areas) and for the period after 1860. What about earlier times and below that level of observation? Eilert Sundt provides the most remarkable and relevant source on the first point. After describing and reflecting upon the regional variations in births out of wedlock, he systematically considers a number of the conditions and practices which appeared to be contributing factors in accounting for that variance. He does so with a kind of detachment remarkable for a man of his time born in Lister deanery – that area, it may be recalled, with the lowest illegitimacy rate in all Norway. The last chapter of his earliest volume devoted to this issue contains an examination of the relationships between "education and good customs" (*Oplysining og gode saeder*). He finds an almost perfect rank correlation between pupil/teacher ratios and the illegitimacy rates as available from reports of the five dioceses then in existence. The first ratio was computed from data for the years 1826, 1837, and 1840, while the illegitimacy rates were derived as reported above. Agder and Bergen diocese reported the lowest number of pupils per teacher, while Tromsø reported the highest number, with Oslo (then including Hamar) at a midpoint between these extremes.[45]

Sundt then limits himself to a closer examination of Agder and Oslo dioceses, since he believes the data are probably more reliable for these two regions. He clusters the fifty-three deaneries into fifteen contiguous groups and then ranks the first seven groups (those within the two dioceses) according to ratio and rate. His second and sixth groups include deaneries within Hedmark and Vest-Agder, respectively, but some beyond their borders. Nevertheless, for present approximations this does not misrepresent the fundamental point too much. Vest-Agder ranks very slightly below Aust-Agder and lower Telemark on the pupil/teacher ratio indicator, with 63 pupils per teacher in 1840. The group containing Hedmark reported the largest number of pupils per teacher for the same year: 103. Further, he compares these seven groups with regard to the percentage of school-age children missing school and finds that group two, including Hedmark, has the highest and group six, including Vest-Agder, the lowest percentages on this indicator of commitment to education around 1840.

Sundt does not claim a direct and unqualified causal relationship between educational commitment and moral conduct. Rather, he traces these contrasts primarily but not exclusively to the intensity and extensity of class cleavage within the populations of these several areas. Where the cleavage is narrow, people share common interests to a greater extent and are more willing to make sacrifices for the common good – in this case, the support of popular education. Where the cleavage is wider, and bitter, such sentiments are weaker. Where, as in Hedmark, land owners dominate the school "boards," sacrifices for mass education are weaker – at least as observed statistically and more personally by Sundt during the 1850s. This willingness to sacrifice is in turn linked to a greater degree of social self-discipline, which in turn partially accounts for the lower illegitimacy rate.

The major relevance of this very partial explication of Sundt's argument is the rather clear-cut contradiction it presents to the educational picture after 1860 when most indicators of educational commitment (except the pupil/teacher ratio) point to Hedmark as more progressive on this dimension than Vest-Agder.

This issue can be refined a bit via presentation of some subprovincial data bearing upon it available for 1861. The first comprehensive report on school conditions following passage of the 1860 school law is, unlike most later reports, organized in terms of deaneries. Just a very few of the more than fifty items of information dealing with teachers, students, and school income and expenditures have been selected and adapted for present purposes in Table 5.8.

These data indicate, first, that the sharp contrast in number of pupils per teacher between the two provinces had been radically narrowed, although Vest-Agder retains a slight favorable edge. It is possible that this ratio had long been a function, in part, of the fact that a higher percentage of pupils in Vest-Agder lived farther from school centers (as indicated by item seven) than in Hedmark. An historical geography of school distribution in this period would be required to check this point. Secondly, the provincial contrast reported in items three (percentage of salaries in kind) and nine (percentage of teachers with more than fifteen years of service) simply sustain the general patterns already discussed above regarding these two indicators of development. Third, average teacher income was consistently and significantly higher

Table 5.8. *Selected attributes of school conditions in the deaneries of Hedmark and Vest-Agder as of 1861*

Selected attributes	Hedmark			Vest-Agder	
	Øster-dalen	Solør og Odalens	Hede-marken	Mandal	Lister
(1) Pupil/teacher ratio	51	71	89	47	49
(2) Average teacher income (RKD)	83	87	65	66	50
(3) Salaries in kind (%)	43	32	29	45	44
(4) Per-pupil expenditures (RKD)	1.13	.75	.77	.95	.53
(5) Pupils **not** instructed in each legally recommended subject (%)	16	21	35	—	38
(6) Pupils instructed **less** than recommended time (%)	45	58	46	4	27
(7) Pupils more than $\frac{1}{4}$ Norwegian mile from school (%)	22	11	5	27	26
(8) Number of pupils receiving private instruction	83	87	64	1	7
(9) Teachers with more than 15 years' service (%)	34	38	30	19	15

Source: See note 3.

in Hedmark, while its per-pupil expenditures average out to a higher figure than Vest-Agder. Next, items five and six clearly point to some kind of discrimination between pupils in terms of the extensity (range of subjects) and intensity (number of school days) available either to them and/or taken advantage of by them. The range of subject-matter data is somewhat ambiguous in that Lister Deanery in Vest-Agder is higher than any of the three Hedmark units, while Mandal appears to have provided all pupils with the full range. On the other hand, item six, showing the percent of pupils instructed less than the recommended time (nine to twelve weeks), is dramatically clear and is certainly not consistent with most of the other indicators. Approximately half of Hedmark's school-age children received less than the recommended time of instruction in 1861, while in Vest-Agder this dropped to 27 percent for Lister and only 4 percent in Mandal Deanery. By 1873, according to the report of that year, these differences had substantially vanished, and both provinces reported figures between 6 and 7 percent. Nevertheless, the 1861 figure is certainly provocative. What does it mean?

The most probable interpretation, it seems to me, is that the children of landless workers, tenant farmers, and perhaps a smaller proportion of lesser landholders were over-represented among those reported as experiencing the shorter period of instruction. This is consistent with Sundt's observations as well as the general tenor of Dokka's discussion of the subject. Furthermore, one of the key demands of the Thrane movement – concentrated, as we have seen, in this province – was precisely more extensive and adequate schooling for their children. Item eight, listing the absolute number of children in private instruction, would seem to be congruent with such an interpretation. It is probable that most if not all those pupils reported in this category were the children of estate owners, large land-owners, or higher officials in provincial administration posts. Studies in comparative education development would also support this view. Elites have seldom been eager to provide their dependent and much-needed labor force with an education which might either provoke further dissatisfaction with their life-situations or facilitate migration to alternative opportunities.

If this interpretation is substantially correct, the most obvious next question is why, after 1860, do all indicators of educational development in Hedmark and the East Country, generally, reveal such an apparent willingness to promote educational improvements? What happened to Vest-Agder's presumably stronger commitment? Some tentative answers to these and other questions related to the social sources of educational development will be attempted in the next and final chapter.

Local history studies of a kind designed to clarify if not really answer questions regarding mass educational experience and popular religious expression at something like a micro level have not, to my knowledge, been undertaken for Norway. If such were ever to be attempted, a focus upon Vest-Agder and an East Country province like Hedmark would provide a particularly promising site for a pilot project, given their striking contrasts on so many of the relevant dimensions as learned from aggregate data comparisons on different levels.[46]

6. Religious diversity and the ambiguity of secularity

We have explored the timing and tempo of educational development and religious change in Norwegian society between about 1740 and 1891, when these reciprocal processes were shaped by some regional contrasts in systems of social stratification. The most fundamental conceptual device in terms of which this descriptive task has been organized is what I label "historical role analysis." This entailed a rather single-minded focus upon the changing role relationships of state-church pastors, parish school teachers, and lay preachers with each other as well as with their parishioners, pupils, parents, and lay-activist audiences. I have been more interested in the course and possible consequences of changes in the social organization of literacy production than in demonstrating the fact of literacy itself. In like fashion, only the most superficial attention has been given to the intellectual/ideological *content* of the several Lutheran theologies, from Orthodoxy through Pietism and Rationalism to Johnsonian Neo-Orthodoxy. These and other such intellectual historical labels were useful points of reference in discussing organizational indicators of diversification in styles of lay and clerical religiosity.

Three major interacting types were distinguished: clerical generations or factions; laicization of religious initiative as organized within the Hauge, Inner- and Outer-Mission movements; and clear-cut sectarian breaks with the established order in contrast to the separations within the church characteristic of the second type. The process of secularization was seen to be intimately related to but distinguishable from these modes of religious diversification in Norwegian society during the period under review. The bulk of our descriptive/analytic attention has been devoted to the progressive laicization of religious leadership in dialectic interplay with shifting emphases in definitions of religiosity from ritual/ideological criteria to experiential requirements of a highly individualized character.

This final chapter will both summarize and extend the discussion thus far. First, an overview of the more central explanatory sketches regarding patterns of religious diversification contained in chapters 2 through 5 will be provided. Secondly, some of the ambiguities of secularity in Norway before 1891 alluded to from time to time throughout the text thus far will be drawn together and extended systematically, using Glock and Stark's five dimensions of religiosity as a kind of negative organizing device.

The laity/clergy ratio as one aspect of historical role analysis[1] can serve as a summary trace element underlying and linking religious diversification and secularization to each other and to the political-economic cross-cleavages which constituted a particularly crucial aspect of the changing context within which these processes developed. As the national aggregate ratio increased from 1,300 to 2,214 between 1750 and 1815, external evidence points to the incipient secularization of elite intellectual life as well as a decline in clerical control over popular styles of religious expression as in the Hauge movement. The ratio was, obviously, a function of elite decisions regarding the allocation of state resources between alternative possibilities and, as such, cannot be taken as an indicator of declining popular religiosity. This qualification on its validity was somewhat relaxed after 1814, when decisions of the newly established Norwegian "Parliament" (Storting) regarding support for the state-church clergy could reflect to some extent the value preferences of enfranchized segments of the male population. Thus, as the ratio increased from 2,214 in 1815 to its nineteenth-century highpoint of 3,164 in 1855, other developments revealed further signs of continued popular laicization and elite secularization, although in somewhat different forms.[2] Differentiation of the professional labor force, initiated during this period via changes at the University of Oslo, ultimately reduced the clergy from the largest to the smallest group within that occupational sector, although only lawyers had surpassed them before 1855. Revocation of the Conventicle Act, Passage of the Dissenter Law, formation of the Norwegian Foreign Mission Society, as well as widespread, rather uncoordinated lay preaching activity, all pointed to a further erosion of the clerical control system and signaled an acceleration in the laicization of religious initiative.

Finally, between 1855 and 1890 the number of laymen per clergyman declined for the first time in over one hundred years, from 3,164 to 2,947 – a trend which did not continue into the twentieth century.[3] The reallocation of resources required to achieve this reversal was prompted both by elite concerns over popular disturbances, whether religious and/or political-economic, as well as a genuine neo-orthodox revival among segments of the elite in a position to influence church economic policy, both in Storting committees and the Ministry of Church and Education. Beginning in the late 1840s that ministry was rather consistently filled by theologically trained men, usually with experience in parish or diocesan church administration – unlike the 1814–1840s period when non-churchmen predominated. This is not to say that elite levels of secularization did not continue to accelerate. On the contrary, most intellectual and social–historical evidence points to the growing structural isolation of the clergy, within the professional labor force and, more generally, as their social recruitment patterns declined, widening still further the life-style gap accentuated by their new styles of religious expression.

Whatever illusions state churchmen may have had about stemming the tide of lay activism via reasserted clerical control made possible by stabilizing and then reducing the ratio's magnitude were obviously shattered by growing lay supremacy within both Outer- and Inner-Mission movement activities. These expanded organizationally at an accelerated rate during the same period the ratio was being reduced.

Obviously, clerical role analysis, however crucial, centers upon only one aspect of a larger system within which certain modes of religious expression are either transmitted and/or transformed. As the conflicts within and between our several clerical generations suggest, the clergy were not always conservative transmitting agents, except in so far as their status prerogatives *vis-à-vis* the laity were concerned. Even this role-set dimension was open to significant self- (and other) redefinition.

It has been argued throughout this essay that the most fateful modifications in Norway's larger religious role system came with the introduction of Confirmation as a fundamentally "new" life-cycle ritual and, above all, the initiation and growth of an ambulatory school system officially designed to implement that objective. The transition from collective catechizing under a parish deacon to individual instruction – however primitive – made possible the social-historical formation of a "plausibility structure" (in Berger's sense) for what I have termed "teacher/laity" religiosity in fluctuating tension with clerical expectations.[4] Given the high turnover rate of ambulatory role occupants, the system generated a continuing supply of incipient parish exegetes, providing a pool from which potentially lay activists were *most likely* to be recruited when other conditions provoked the need for nonclerical leadership. Admittedly, this assertion, so crucial to part of my argument, remains a plausible but empirically precarious assumption in the absence of more adequate research on the occupational pasts of many such local-level leaders, whether religious or (as we shall note) political after about 1833.

On the other hand, as seminarians began to displace parish-trained catechists, their more extended religious education reinforced and (or?) created the popular image of a kind of quasi-professional theologian located somewhere between lay activists and university-trained clergymen in a scale of symbolic skills. As these teachers moved from farm homes to schoolhouses after 1860 and the process of professionalization accelerated, as indicated by certification, declining turnover rates, and a progressive shift from payment in kind to cash, their growing self-consciousness as a relatively distinct occupational status group was significantly enhanced. To repeat, such developments in the organization of literacy production, particularly when extended by a more differentiated curriculum, provided the social foundations for that teacher/laity religiosity in variable tension with the more disciplined styles of religious expression within lay activist circles "below" and the clergy "above."

As we have seen, this religiosity could move in *at least* three directions. First and most dramatically, it could and did provide the generative base for lay-activist leadership. Second, and not sufficiently emphasized earlier, it could and probably most frequently did reinforce clerical expectations *vis-à-vis* the laity in ways formally and originally intended by school reform legislation. Finally, it could provide a pool of incipient secular ideologues more likely and able to articulate those social reconstructions of reality required by the political/economic and demographic disruptions particularly after about 1860.

Once again, it has been my objective to construct a partial explanation for some regional variations in the timing and tempo, as well as intensity and extensity, of these processes of religious change by relating them to the timing and tempo of certain "independent" transformations in both the clerical and educational role systems. Let us go on now to a very brief summary of those interplays.

First, neo-orthodox parish clergymen trained under the influence of Gisle Johnson and the awakening associated with him displaced an earlier, less evangelically aggressive clerical generation between 1850 and 1875. I have asserted, on an assumption about seniority prerogatives, that this displacement process occurred first on the periphery (Agder, Bergen, Tromso dioceses) and tended to occur later in Oslo, Hamar, and Trondhjem. Concurrently, the social origins of this new breed moved downward into our lower-middle stratum, closer to but still distanced from that of common school teachers.

Secondly, while significant changes in the training of the rural educational labor force began in the 1830s, it accelerated most dramatically after the School Law of 1860. Here, unlike the case of the clergy, the regional displacement pattern was reversed. That is, the transition from ambulatory to fixed schools as well as some additional signs of incipient professionalization occurred first and most rapidly in the East Country dioceses and later, as well as more slowly, in the west and, above all, southwest.

Third, laicization, as partially indicated by the Inner Mission's growth pattern, accelerated most notably after 1868. Once again, this lay mobilization was not a regionally uniform process. Organizational indicators, both vertical (provincial and other associations of locals) and horizontal (absolute and relative number of locals as related to population size), revealed earliest and most rapid growth in the west-southwest and later, slower movement in the east-central parishes.

Finally, I have argued that these regional variations in the timing of clerical displacement patterns and educational change, mediated by contrasting systems of power, privilege, and prestige, partially account for regional variations in levels of lay mobilization. That is, higher mobilization in the egalitarian west was enhanced by an early influx of Johnsonian clergy and delayed educational change. In contrast, sharp class polarization in the eastern parishes, combined with early and rapid educational change which preceded displacement of the pre-Johnsonian clerical generation, were among the conditions which inhibited the mobilization process.

Historical sociologists of religion until rather recently have tended to neglect the empirical study of laicization within established systems. Case studies of sectarian movements combined with a continued proliferation and/or repudiation of typologies designed to comprehend their social historical variety remain, perhaps, the most popular within the field.[5] The two phenomena are, of course, intimately related, as Joachim Wach observed many years ago as part of his typological refinements of individual and collective protest within religious systems.[6]

More recently, Werner Stark and Michael Hill have devoted substantial studies to the preconditions and processes whereby religious orders (in the monastic sense) proliferated in Christendom and appear to have contained incipient sectarian breaks within established patterns of control.[7] It may be suggested that these orders often have been lay initiatives ultimately coopted by clerical control systems, while laicization as used here refers to a reversal of that relationship, i.e., where the clergy/laity conflict issues in a kind of mutual cooptation but with lay dominance.

The magnitude of clear-cut sectarian separatism in Norway by 1891, a bit less than 1.5 percent of the national population, was probably among the lowest in northwestern Europe. A reliable historical geography of religious pluralism on a comparative continental scale might support that assertion. Moreover, less than one-third of these dissenters were organized within a group which might reasonably be regarded as "indigenous," i.e., the Lutheran

Free Church. This remarkably low level of "sectarian productivity," in spite of conditions which elsewhere have been associated with its proliferation, is one of the most interesting features of the Norwegian case. For example, Stark's thesis that established state church (*caesaropapist*) systems are particularly generative of sectarian breaks, while the presumed greater autonomy of the Roman Catholic Church in its several political contexts is much less so, would have to be re-examined in light of this variant, and indeed the Scandinavian cases more generally.[8]

Haugeanism provides a particularly instructive example for deviant case analysis in the sociology of sectarianism. Initially, particularly between 1796 and 1804, the movement exhibited a number of classical sectarian attributes which at other times and places had been associated with ultimate separatism. Yet it became, in the Norwegian context, what I have elsewhere labeled an "incipient sect." Phillip Hammond has regarded Haugeanism among Norwegian immigrants to the United States after 1840 as a "migrating sect."[9] This apparent contradiction is, I submit, only partial. That is, Haugeanism in America became one of several synods competing for immigrant loyalties. One of these, Det Norske Synode (The Norwegian Synod) approximated the state church most closely in its territorial organization and, above all, its insistence upon certain clerical prerogatives in religious affairs. During this same period back in Norway (*c.* 1840 to 1868), the movement was being "absorbed" by the much larger, more pervasive, and systematically organized mission movement, both Inner and Outer, in the founding of which Haugeans had played leading roles.

This apparent retention capacity is further suggested by the fact that the two largest dissenter bodies in 1891 (Lutheran Free Church and Methodists) were very close in styles of religiosity to those lay-activist groups which remained within the state church. We have already noted the exogenous origins of all but the Free Church movement among the separatist population, and even here external stimuli may well have been decisive. An earlier cleavage within the established Church of Scotland was explicitly cited as a precedent by the two state-church ministers who resigned their posts to lead the movement.

In summary, the overall picture conveyed both by laicization within and separation from the Norwegian religious establishment is one of normative tension and particularistic objection, rather than the more radical breaks with prevailing styles of religious expression so often found in more pluralistic societies of non-Catholic Europe and America. Most observers have attributed this phenomenon to a combination of symbolic isolation and, above all, the fundamental success of preparation for Confirmation in Pontoppidan

Confessionalism as an indoctrinating device together with the pervasive internalization and consequent social psychological function of Confirmation as a life-cycle rite of passage, particularly during the preindustrial period.[10]

The ambiguity of secularity

The dissolution of religious unity in Norwegian society, which accelerated after 1850, included, in addition to the patterns of diversification summarized above, a process of secularization which, like its awakening counterpart, was differentially distributed regionally and in social space. Our attention to this phenomenon has been recurrent but scattered throughout the discussion thus far. It is now my intention to draw together these observations and at the same time extend the discussion systematically in order to reduce some of the ambiguity which is too often associated with this concept – at least in the Norwegian context.

The literature on secularization probably has been more voluminous than on any other single theme in the scientific study of religion during the last twenty-five years or so. As I have tried to suggest in the introduction, much of this attention has been devoted to seemingly endless and often rather sterile conceptual refinements and disputes. Longitudinal, as opposed to cross-sectional, studies of religiosity with explicit empirical indicators designed to clarify some conception of secularization as an historical process over particular times and places are, by contrast, very few indeed.[11] Peter Berger's definition of and historical/contemporary reflection upon secularization in his *The Sacred Canopy* are both reasonably clear and rather "conventional," if such a word can be applied to a body of literature which seems to possess few, if any, conventions. By "secularization" he refers to the "process by which sectors of society and culture are removed from the domination of religious institutions and symbols."[12] This abstract phrasing, I submit, is congruent with my deliberately "concrete" limiting definition of that process as the decline of a historically specific religious order (e.g., Norway's in 1741–1891) as an independent and/or contingent variable in social conduct, process, and change.

Glock and Stark's five dimensions of religiosity provide a practical framework within which historical evidence bearing on that process may be reviewed and extended systematically. Representative historical evidence directly relevant to the construction of empirical indicators along each of these dimensions is simply nonexistent. This holds particularly for the intellectual and ritual dimensions. On the other hand, indirect indicators of ideological secularity may be constructed on the basis of historical ecological studies of voting behavior on the basis of certain assumptions to be spelled out below. Most of the following discussion will, therefore, be devoted to the political context of the ideological dimension, with a few plausible inferences regarding the experiential implications of that same data. Some fragmentary evidence related to the political orientations of parish school teachers will be included in that discussion. Finally, the logic underlying historical role analysis will be utilized in a brief review of the evidence on consequential secularization.

First, measured along the intellectual dimension (i.e., the social distribution of knowledge of a sacred literature, doctrine, etc.), all evidence points to a massive increase in levels of religiosity between 1740 and 1891, at least at the popular level. A basic training in Pontoppidan's "systematic theology" was later supplemented by exposure to Bible and church history. On the other hand, the common school curriculum expanded and the range of popular literature differentiated to include a much wider range of secular topics. This could issue in a kind of incipient intellectual secularization without actually reducing the level of formal Christian knowledge significantly.

Class-determined variations in the range and content of educational experiences were marked by an expansion in the proportion of upper- and upper-middle strata participation in secondary- and university-level training. As we have seen, secularization of the professional labor force was related to a decline in theological faculty enrollments, both as preparation for a clerical career and as a background for secondary level teaching positions. Contrariwise, given the continuing relative educational deprivation of Eastern Norway's stratum of tenant farmers and agricultural workers, it seems probable that their level of basic intellectual religiosity was the lowest outside of north Norway. Nevertheless, the overall trend on this dimension, while possibly on a downward slope after about 1860 as literal memorization of Pontoppidan began to be de-emphasized, can hardly be described as secular in contrast to conditions before 1740. This rather simplistic interpretation of this indicator neglects a recurrent historical pattern. Increased religious knowledge has often provided the symbolic resources for internal diversification, which in turn has been related to overt expressions of indifference, skepticism, and/or repudiation of at least some elements of the traditional system.

Participation in life-cycle and annual ritual occasions within voluntaristic systems provides a reasonably valid indicator of one aspect of religious commitment. Church discipline reinforced by legal sanctions made baptism, confirmation, marriage, and funeral ceremonies compulsory liturgical events, thereby raising obvious doubts about the utility of this measure until some time after 1891. On the other hand, as we have seen, the neo-Orthodox

Johnsonian clergy tried, unsuccessfully, to make such participation voluntary, with the proviso that they could define preconditions for admission to them. They hoped to exploit traditional commitments to these ritual occasions as a coercive device in forcing ideological/experiential conformity. There is little or no evidence which suggests that participation in these occasions would have declined significantly in the absence of formal legal requirements. Just what individual and collective enactment of these events meant to the participants is another matter. Here, rather substantial if anecdotal accounts point to the ritual system as the bedrock of a folk religiosity, elements of which predated both conversion to Christianity and, more certainly, the Reformation. When lay and clerical activists condemned "educated Christianity" (more literally, *opdragelseskristendom* could be translated as "brought-up Christianity"), they referred as much or more to reliance on passive ritual participation than to the intellectual achievements just discussed.

Church attendance and participation in Communion fluctuated over time and regionally in ways not possible for life-cycle cultic episodes. Not so paradoxically, as attendance rose during the popular revival, participation in Communion declined. Molland is certainly correct in attributing this to the scare tactics of Johnsonian clerics who declared that partaking of the Sacrament without the required spiritual qualifications was to "eat and drink oneself to damnation." The dramatic decline, strangely unanticipated by those responsible for it, could almost be interpreted as evidence of a heightened ideological/experiential sensitivity rather than as part of a secularizing trend. Once the revival tapered off and a new generation of less demanding clerics attempted to increase participation, the earlier levels were, apparently, never again regained.[13]

Unlike these first two dimensions, historical evidence describing regional variations over time in degrees of ideological or experiential religiosity are not a matter of public record – except very indirectly. More fundamental to the controversy over secularization as a useful concept in the study of religious change has been the inclusion of experiential criteria as, depending on the analyst, more or less central to the determination of secularity. Except for a spiritual elite of religious virtuosi within medieval Catholicism (e.g., some members of religious orders, saints, etc.), this standard was not applied to the judgment of mass religiosity in Norway until the appearance of Pietism and the diffusion of Haugean expectations after 1800. When religiosity has been construed in this narrow fashion it is hardly surprising that some critics of secularization as a concept in empirical study have argued that "religious decline" is not only a myth, but that in reality the direction of change has been precisely the reverse. That is, there were or are a larger number of "genuine" Christians in nineteenth- or twentieth-century France (or England, or Norway) than there were in the Age of Faith (thirteenth century). Another variant on this position leads to the idea that Europe was not really converted to Christianity until the advent of left-wing Evangelical Protestantism. Obviously, when used in this single-factor fashion, experiential criteria are simply useless in comparative historical study. If, on the other hand, we start with the Thomas Theorem that what men define as real is real in its consequences, then the empirical task becomes discovering the extent to which experiential criteria are accepted among the unawakened. This would entail the acceptance of the historical relativity of popular conceptions of religiosity, including their internal contradictions and, as here, their multi-dimensional character.

These issues may be explored further by a consideration of presumed changes in the ideological dimension of Norwegian religious life up to about 1891. From a Johnsonian point of view, some variations on experiential requirements were regarded as one aspect of orthodox Lutheranism, here regarded as the core of our ideological descriptive focus.

Two partially overlapping historical trace elements are most relevant here. Grundtvigianism in church and school, and the bourgeois political left (*venstre*). Gisle Johnson's archenemies within the clergy had been those men most influenced by humanistic elements within Grundtvigianism among the previous clerical generation trained under Hersleb and Stenersen and "led" by Wexels in Oslo. Given Johnson's control over theological training after 1850, as well as his preeminent authority within the home-mission movement, these opponents were either isolated or gradually eliminated from all levels of state-church administration. Just how numerous and/or influential this faction actually was before and after 1850 is not clear from the literature.[14] Comparable efforts to purge them from the educational system were apparently less successful, despite progressive neo-Orthodox control over the central administration as well as diocesan teacher-training seminaries.

Norway's major educational reformers of the mid and late nineteenth century were powerfully influenced by Grundtvig's educational philosophy. Their pedagogic theory and practice presupposed an optimistic view of human nature and destiny which Professor Johnson attacked as the most pernicious of all errors promoted by his opponents. He was no doubt correct in assessing the insidious potential of these ideas to fundamental Lutheran doctrine (such as belief in Original Sin, upon which so many other elements rested). From this perspective, in so far as seminarians were actually influenced by these views in the content and style of their parish level teaching, we might regard them, on this dimension, as secularizing agents. The Johnsonians clearly did so.

Another look at regional variations in the timing and tempo of LF's mobilization pattern is helpful in this connection. As Johnsonian clerics moved into the east inland parishes they encountered ideological/experiential indifference and, at best, ritual/intellectual passivity. As we have seen, outright hostility was a more likely response from tenant farmers and agricultural workers. Marcus Thrane's personal religiosity was at least partially congruent with ethical/humanistic Grundtvigian themes prevalent among many teachers and pre-Johnsonian pastors whose influence was greater here than in the coastal parishes of the west-southwestern dioceses.[15] Given the early, rapid, and more extensive educational development in the east, combined with the delayed displacement by Johnsonians of the previous clerical generation, it seems plausible to conclude that the Johnsonian impact was systematically inhibited even before it began. To what extent their formal control of educational and religious role system decision-making after about 1870 enabled them to reduce such market resistance is not clear.

Crudely summarized, if the Johnsonians' insistence upon Confessional purity (*ritus vocatus*) lost them control of West Country activists, it simply alienated an already unreceptive East Country laity still further. Given the dramatic contrast in mobilizing success between Thrane and LF in this area, we may infer that both Bible Messengers and Johnsonian pastors found it very difficult to promote original sin and salvation as a substitute for social justice. Grundtvigian-inspired efforts to bring sweetness, light, and more instrumental learning to these provinces with a view to enhancing human dignity and Norwegian national identity was probably more acceptable. Insofar as pastors, teachers, and lay preachers working in the Hamar diocese found it necessary to attack these "Lutheran Revisionist" efforts, the ensuing ideological polarization, analogous to its political–economic counterpart, may have mobilized hitherto passive segments of the laity to active "disbelief" (*vantro*), certainly as defined by Johnsonian criteria of experiential/ideological religiosity. Our brief sketch of selected religious and educational conditions in the Hamar Diocese deaneries of Østerdalen, Hedemarken, Solør and Odalen in chapter 5 would seem to sustain these inferences.

The cleavages which issued from these continuing conflicts as well as those within the Inner-Mission movement itself reflected and interacted with those stemming from concurrent political mobilization patterns in the bitter struggle for and against parliamentary government before 1884.[16] The regionally variable linkages between these two processes have been described with quantitative clarity by Stein Rokkan, his associates, and others in impressive historical–ecological studies of partisan mobilization in Norwegian politics, particularly since 1882 when reliable voting statistics first become available.[17]

Rodney Stark, in a comparative study of religion and radical politics, found rather consistent support for the proposition that "within any given political system persons supporting parties on the left would be less involved in religion than those supporting rightist parties."[18] This familiar relationship between political radicalism and alienation from or indifference to an established religious order can be shown to hold, with certain crucial qualifications, for the Norwegian scene between from 1868 and beyond 1891. Election statistics, assuming the validity of this association, provide an indirect indicator of ideological aspects of religiosity which can be interpreted in the context of more qualitative evidence.

Organized mass movements for the attainment of political–economic objectives appeared most notably after 1845, as in the Thrane movement. Partisan organizations for the exercise of influence in the electoral and legislative processes appeared later and were necessarily restricted in their formal composition to economically qualified strata within a restricted suffrage system. Stein Rokkan observes that the enfranchized segments of the peasantry

moved much more cautiously [than Thrane] and did not develop a nationwide network of political associations until 1865. These "Friends of the Peasants" reached a membership of some 21,000 and spread to the South and West as well as the East. The primary aim of the association was to influence the voters and the electors in the rural constituencies and to ensure the election of trusted opponents of the officials and the King's government. The leader of the urban opposition, Johan Sverdrup, soon saw the importance of this movement and established an alliance in 1869. This was the first step toward the formation of a united opposition party, the Left, as it soon came to be called, and it also marked the beginning of the great struggle for power in the Norwegian system.[19]

It is, perhaps, not entirely coincidental that Inner-Mission mobilization, which ran concurrently with these political developments, attempted national coordination of its efforts through LF just one year earlier, 1868. Given Professor Johnson's pivotal role as initiator and mediator, his response to these developments provides the best single source of insight into the interplay between religious and political forms of collective action. There is little if any doubt that when he formulated the Emergency Principle as a strategic device in the struggle against disbelief, indifference, and sectarianism, what became the political left represented for him a, if not the, major social expression of that crisis. Its challenge to traditional authority contained in the doctrine of popular sovereignty and the correlative conception of human nature was condemned as a fundamental expression of disbelief (*vantro*). Johnson's Lutheran Confessionalism pervaded his political philosophy and remained reasonably consistent throughout his career, from the initial and continuing attacks on Grundtvigianism among clergymen and school teachers in the 1850s to his probable authorship of the famous *Manifesto to the Friends of Christianity in Our Land* in 1883.[20]

Religious components in the ongoing political conflicts after 1869 surfaced with greatest clarity during the constitutional crises of the 1880s, when partisan loyalties between Left and Right (*Høyre*) were formally organized in provincial associations.[21] The Left in its drive toward parliamentary government steadily increased its Storting majorities until 1882, when over two-thirds of that body was committed to the one unifying goal of impeaching the royal cabinet and forcing the King to choose all future cabinets from among the Storting majority. This massive threat to an established order, which, despite revocation of the Conventicle Act in 1841, had guaranteed predominant clerical control over religious and educational affairs, triggered the attempt by Gisle Johnson and his co-workers to exploit religious cleavages for political ends. Their major strategy was to split the opposition by emphasizing the dramatic religious diversity within the Left's coalition, which ranged from West Country radical lay activists to Eastern and urban "Free Thinkers." This desperate rear-guard action not only proved politically counter-productive but also crystalized new and reinforced old varieties of anti-clericalism, which were only partially reduced by a sequence of concessions to lay demands for extended democracy in church affairs.

Once parliamentary rule was established (1884), the precarious coalition constructed by the Left for that overriding objective collapsed. There was simply no longer an issue or combination of issues sufficiently powerful to reconcile its internal ideological tensions. It split almost precisely along those lines which the Conservatives had hoped to exploit by means of Johnson's (and LF's) presumed influence among religious activists. Rokkan and Valen's succinct description and interpretation of this process is directly relevant to our concerns: the Left

split up into a "Pure Wing" of radical nationalists and a "Moderate" wing of spokesmen for traditional religious and moral values. This split cut across earlier territorial cleavages and produced a temporary alliance between Conservatives and the centre and fundamentalists in the periphery. The "Moderates" were concentrated in the South-West: they had their only urban strongholds in the cities of Stavanger and Haugesund and they derived most of their support from the coastal communities in that region. The contrasts between these outer districts and the agricultural communities in the inner fjords and valleys were indeed striking and there is much evidence to suggest that the differences between "Moderates" and "Pures" in fact reflected contrasts in community norms and traditional ethical attitudes.[22]

The relationship between these political developments and our central concern with popular religiosity and, by indirection, ideological secularity are of most immediate relevance here. LF's attempt to mobilize the religious periphery into a single national organization without repudiating the centralist *ritus vocatus* doctrine reflected an almost desperate blindness to social–historical realities. We may surmise that it was kept in a state of suspended animation only in the minds of Johnson and other clerical LF tacticians. On the other hand, their high-church clerical critics inisted that it was alive and well, confessionally if not sociologically, while bitterly attacking lay activists who, without conceding its Biblical birth, obviously decided it was dead and behaved accordingly.

The struggle for Inner-Mission unity, as indicated by regional variations in the timing and tempo with which locals and/or associations affiliated nationally, corresponded in part to concurrent patterns of political coalition formation and dissolution. The affiliation tempo accelerated after 1884 and reached a temporary climax during the same period when the Christian Left formed a transitory alliance with their earlier Conservative opponents in state, church, and Inner-Mission affairs. Given the exigencies of this bargaining process, it seems hardly coincidental that LF changed its symbolically unacceptable name (i.e., from the Luther Foundation to the Norwegian Inner-Mission Society) and publicly dropped Johnson's Emergency Principle in 1891, an election year.

Given this political split between lay activists and the Johnsonian clergy, what can be said about those teachers who stood between and among them as primary transmitters of Christian and (increasingly) other knowledge which might clarify the range of ideological orientations within that educational role system? Most of the evidence, both direct and inferential, points to an alliance with *venstre* for a significant majority. This in turn might suggest the presence among them of lay activists in the west and southwest, on the one hand, and possible Grundtvigian, folk-high-school-style advocates in the *fjell* (mountain), fjord and eastern valley regions, on the other. Given their social origins and probable upward mobility analogous to other strata mobilizing on the Left, combined with the more tangible fact that this party pushed through the first major salary reform (and increase) for all parish school teachers up to that time, this assertion seems warranted.

Parish school teachers were increasingly prominent at all levels of political representation, rural communal councils (after 1837) and small towns or cities to the Storting. The most obvious cases in the Storting during this period were Ole Gabrielle Ueland, chieftain of the peasant contingent, and Søren Jaabek, founder and leader of that "Friends of the Peasant" movement mentioned by Rokkan above. Ueland had been a teacher and *kirkensanger* (deacon) in Rogaland. Jaabek's career included a stint as ambulatory school teacher in Vest-Agder, with later activity as an editor. Moreover, given the high turnover rate among common school teachers and the fact that seminary or other teacher-training centers provided the only accessible form of general education beyond the common school, ex-teachers and incipient teachers simply disappeared into other occupational categories. That process obscured the actual magnitude of this source of peasant leadership, whether religious or political. Ueland, to name but one of the most prominent examples, was both.

All this is not to claim that teachers constituted a very cohesive status group. According to Dokka, their life-situations remained sufficiently diverse, regionally and otherwise, to inhibit united political action even on some school issues.[23] Such diversity could stem, in part, from ideological religiosity cleavages reflecting those "contrasts in community norms and traditional ethical attitudes" to which Rokkan and Valen referred above. Insofar as teachers and/or deacons became spokesmen for such localized orientations beyond their own parishes, cross regional unities would probably often be inhibited. On the other hand, it is important to emphasize that after seminaries and other teacher-training centers began to displace the strictly home-grown, parochial Confirmation-class product with their more sophisticated trainees, patterns of career mobility also changed. These men began to resemble the clergy in still another way, in that they were, more often than not, outsiders. That is, in so far as teaching actually became their life career it was likely to take them away from their home parish. Given the prevalence of such a pattern, teachers became agents of change as well as continuity for reasons even more fundamental than their professional training and role development.

As this educational labor force was politicized on the Left, and in so far as this brought them into still another area of conflict with their clerical parish superiors who were mobilized overwhelmingly on the Right, the tensions generated between them, as well as in their respective relationships to pupils, parents, and lay preachers, could hardly have facilitated the uncritical transmission of "community norms and traditional ethical attitudes." At other times and places, such stresses and strains within networks of human sociation have generated symbolic pluralism as earlier definitions of social reality were called in question and a wider range of alternative possibilities became accessible, above all, via an ever more-effective mass literacy.

Just what ideological options became attitudinal and behavioral realities regionally and at the parish level remains a matter of inference based on the kind of scattered evidence I have pointed to throughout the text, i.e., LF affiliation patterns, sectarian distributions, Left/Right vote distributions, etc. To this it might have been helpful to add the distribution of folk high schools in the Grundtvigian tradition.

Given these obvious data limitations, what can be said in summary about the social distribution of ideological secularity? If our criteria of "disbelief" were to be overt militant atheism, the answer would be "infinitesimal." At the other extreme, if we accepted hard-core lay activist definitions in which experiential criteria were almost co-terminous with ideological requirements, something over ninety percent of the population would be instant secularists, or at best somnambulent Christians. Gisle Johnson and his clerical followers were apparently somewhat less stringent, at least during the political crises of the 1880s, and seemed to admit the political Right (*Høyre*) into the ranks of believers. This view was explicitly and often bitterly repudiated by lay activists, who pointed to local conservatives as among the leading disbelievers in their communities.[24]

Perhaps the simplest "solution" to this problem would be to reverse Glock and Stark's fifth dimension of religiosity (the *consequential*) and ask what outward signs of an inward secularity can be specified. First, in chapter 1, we examined the rationale underlying religious role analysis in general and the laity/clergy ratio in particular, as a way of getting at the relative and changing value placed upon a social historically specific tradition within a given society's value hierarchy. Insofar as that indicator is regarded as partially valid, it certainly points in a secularizing direction. Secondly, *if* lawyers, doctors, natural scientists, humanistic scholars, literary men, and other artists are seen as agents of "normative humanism," then the differentiation of Norway's professional labor force during the nineteenth century can be interpreted as a further dimension of "consequential secularity," at least for those strata within the orbit of their professional influence. This assertion does not require the assumption that these men explicitly repudiated orthodox doctrines which contradicted or were in tension with their own presup-positions. Whatever secularizing impact their professional role enactment had was, no doubt, more often than not unintentional – the unanticipated consequence of occupational routines. Their personal styles of religious expression were probably most commonly limited to life-cycle cultic occasions.

The most overt historically visible secularizing agents in Norway during this period were certainly, as noted in chapter 4, literary men such as Ibsen, Bjørnsen, Kjelland, Garborg, Vinje and, starting just after 1891, the younger

Knut Hamsun. Just how extensive and intensive their normative impact may have been is very problematic indeed. A systematic quantitative historical description of the volume and distribution of their work has not, so far as I know, been done. It is probable that their market was concentrated in urban areas (though weak in Stavanger and Haugesund?) within upper and upper-middle strata and most frequently among those readers on the secular Left. Significant contact with labor movement activists was probably limited most notably to Oslo and other East Country urban centers.

Finally, the most accessible and persuasive evidence of proletarian secularity is, once again, organizational. Thrane's short-lived success in worker mobilization was almost but not quite totally rural (i.e., among agricultural workers, tenant farmers, etc.). As urbanization began to accelerate after about 1850, something resembling a modern industrial labor force began to appear in a modest way. Its magnitude fluctuated considerably until after 1891, reflecting concurrent variations in market conditions shaped both by domestic and international economic exchange patterns. Transient signs of an incipient socialist labor movement appeared and faded away in the 1870s and 1880s. The first sustained trade union organizational network which transcended particular localities was not firmly established until 1898.

The relationship between most if not all of these worker associations and the clergy seems to have been at best one of suspicion, but more frequently overt hostility. The East Country urban working class was recruited from that rural proletariat of tenant farmers and landless laborers described earlier. Given the combination of their relatively low level of intellectual religiosity stemming from a less effective and sustained educational experience and the fact that the laity/clergy ratio was several times larger in rapidly urbanizing areas than in their home parishes, the ideological impact of labor movement leadership was certainly more likely to be successful than, for example, that of Inner-Mission activists. If so, the further erosion of an already precarious ideological religiosity probably accelerated as one aspect of the urban industrial–political mobilization process. This probability has been regarded as almost a social historical truism by some scholars. The "de-Christianization" of the European working class is just one of those things that "everybody knows." Critics of the secularization concept have pointed to a tendency on the part of radical intellectuals to recreate proletarian experiential/ideological worlds in their own images, while orthodox religionists seem chronically given to "viewing with alarm." Neither perspective provides representative empirical evidence of proletarian opinion. Nevertheless, while this issue deserves a more careful reexamination, the weight of current evidence is certainly in a secularizing direction.

My emphasis throughout this book has been upon the consequences of educational development for patterns of lay mobilization and styles of religiosity. The reverse relationship has not been ignored, but we may usefully close our consideration of that interplay with a brief review of some of the more salient points. First, most observers would agree that Lutheran Pietism was the single most crucial force initiating the push toward mass literacy for religious ends. Practical appeals were always blended in the otherwise religious rhetoric of both Pietist and, to a greater extent, Rationalist Lutheran advocates of popular literacy. In reality the overwhelming focus on Pontoppidan in the rural ambulatory system indicates that whatever practical consequences that experience may have had was an incidental by-product of preparation for confirmation.

Once the process of lay mobilization was triggered in Pietist Conventicals, Haugean circles, Inner- and Outer-Mission locals, as well as diverse separatist groups, an informal organizational context of immense importance to the production and/or reinforment of functional literacy came into a sustained existence. As we have seen, the single most popular and widespread label for these activists among their more passive neighbors was that of "readers." Above all, they continued to read even after Confirmation, when, within the rural economy, it was hardly necessary and could be expensive.

Lawrence Stone has argued that "the rivalry of the various Christian churches and sects for control of men's minds did more to stimulate education in the West between 1550 and 1850 than any other single factor."[25] He is referring primarily to England and other regions within western European nation states where such pluralism had developed between Catholics and Protestants, Dissenters and Anglicans, etc. Norway does not present such a case of obvious, clear-cut pluralism. Less than two percent of the population was outside the state church by 1891, and to this day it is less than ten percent. Nevertheless, it may be argued that a kind of factional pluralism within surface unity has functioned in a somewhat comparable fashion if not with quite the same intensity. For example, the struggle between Orthodox, Pietist, and Rationalist clergy certainly issued in a more or less intense struggle for the popular mind which was partially expressed within the parish school system, in a way, perhaps, not unlike that between Evangelicals, Latitudinarians, and Apostolicals within the Church of England. The incipient pluralism inherent within such intra-church conflict was even more evident in the tensions between Haugeans and their opponents, Inner-Mission activists and their detractors.

The clearest case of intra-church competition issuing in educational consequences was that between Grundtvigians and Johnsonians, which overlapped to a notable extent with that between lay activists and their opponents. This entailed a struggle for control over the national parish school system. Grundtvigian-inspired folk high schools and teacher-training centers were regarded as a major threat by the Johnsonians, and, as we have seen, a concerted campaign was launched to eliminate or at least neutralize their influence. This process in turn overlapped with and expanded into a more general, and as seen in the previous section, rather ambiguous conflict between diverse varieties of "religionists" on the one side and comparably variable "secularists" on the other. This was expressed on the political and literary fronts as well as in disputes over educational policy.

We have come full circle back to our several points of departure in the mutually reinforcing interplay between lay mobilization, secularization, and educational development. Cutting into the flow of Norwegian history between 1740 and 1891, I have tried to specify some regional variations in the timing and tempo of that three-way interaction. Obviously this dialectic process continued after 1891. Above all, as large-scale industrial enterprises began to concentrate large numbers of workers in single locations and organized political cleavages proliferated after the introduction of universal male suffrage in 1899, all three processes accelerated. Parish-level voluntary associations, in spite of their internal cleavages and conflicts, became even more dominant in popular definitions of religiosity – above all in the inner meaning of what constituted a "believing Christian."[26] The varieties of secular experience and expression continued to differentiate in multileveled ways within and between the Marxist socialist parties on the Left and the fragmenting bourgeois parties variably located somewhere on the Right, and this political dimension of secularity was only one of several. Educational policy formation inevitably had to reconcile an ever wider range of conflicting values, values which in turn continued to impinge upon and partially sustain the other processes.

Notes

Preface

1 J. T. Flint, "A Handbook for Historical Sociologists," *Comparative Studies in Society and History*, vol. 10, no. 4, July 1968, pp. 492–509.

2 I prefer the words "explanatory sketch" to "theory" since I continue to share George Homans' rather rigorous, formal criteria when using the latter term. It is now almost impossible to avoid the casual use of the word "theory," however ambiguous its reference, since the term pervades the literature. I will, therefore, not be consistent in the present work. See George C. Homans, "Contemporary Theory in Sociology," in R. E. L. Faris (ed.), *Handbook of Modern Sociology*, Rand McNally, Chicago, 1964, pp. 951–977 and p. 495.

3 J. T. Flint, "Conceptual Translations in Comparative Study," *Comparative Studies in Society and History*, vol. 18, no. 4, October 1976, pp. 509–512.

1 Introduction

1 C. A. Anderson and Mary Jean Bowman (eds.), *Education and Economic Development*, Aldine, Chicago, 1963; James S. Coleman (ed.), *Education and Political Development*, Princeton University Press, Princeton, 1965; Frederick Harbison and Charles A. Myers, *Education, Manpower, and Economic Growth*, McGraw-Hill, New York, 1964.

2 *Carlo M. Cipolla, Literacy and Development in the West*, Penguin Books, Baltimore, Maryland, 1969; R. P. Dore, *Education in Tokugawa Japan*, University of California Press, Berkeley, 1965; Lawrence Stone, "Japan and England, A Comparative Study," reprinted in P. W. Musgrave (ed.), *Sociology, History and Education*, Methuen & Co., London, 1970; Harvey J. Graff, *The Literacy Myth: Literacy and Social Structure in the 19th Century City*, Academic Press, New York, 1979.

3 Max Weber, "The Sociology of Religion," chapter 6 in Guenther Roth and Claus Wittich (eds.), *Economy and Society*, Bedminster Press, New York, 1968.

   Noah and Eckstein attempted to assess the relationship between other-worldly orientations and educational emphasis using contemporary aggregate data. Their inconclusive findings for the current scene cannot, it seems to me, be applied without reservations for periods before economic developments altered this hypothesized relationship. See H. J. Noah and M. A. Eckstein, *Toward a Science of Comparative Education*, Macmillan, London, 1969. The question must remain open.

   An impressive micro-historical study which directly challenges some of these assertions came to my attention after the completion of this manuscript: R. A. Houston, *Scottish Literacy and Scottish Identity: Illiteracy and Society in Scotland and Northern England, 1600–1800*, Cambridge University Press, Cambridge, 1985. There is of course, a very sizeable and still growing literature on this phenomenon which would have to be taken into account in any expansion of my present focus to include, for example, Sweden, Colonial New England, France, etc. My concern is not with literacy as such but rather the social organization of its production.

 4 This set of conceptual linkages derives from my modification of and extension of several sources but particularly Hans Gerth and C. Wright Mills, *Character and Social Structure*, Harcourt, Brace and World, New York, 1953. Wherever quotation marks appear in the next few paragraphs of text without direct attribution the words are drawn from this source. Also see Peter L. Berger, *The Sacred Canopy*, Doubleday Anchor, New York, 1967; Terrence K. Hopkins and Immanuel Wallerstein, "Research Proposal: Patterns of Development of the Modern World System," *Review* vol. 1, no. 2, Fall 1977, pp. 111–145; and Immanuel Wallerstein, *The Modern World-System*, Academic Press, New York, 1974. See also Flint, "A Handbook for Historical Sociologists."

 5 Wallerstein, *World System*; Hopkins and Wallerstein, "Research Proposal."

 6 Robert Wuthnow, "World Order and Religious Movements," in Bergesen, Albert (ed.), *Studies of the Modern World System*, Academic Press, New York, 1980, pp. 57–75.

 7 Berger, *Sacred Canopy*.

 8 Karel Dobbelaere, "Secularization: A Multi-Dimensional Concept," *Current Sociology*, vol. 29, no. 2, Summer 1981, pp. 1–215. It is not my concern here to provide yet another critique of a critique of a concept but rather to attempt the construction of some social–historical indicators of that sub-type of religious change which I label "secularization" as defined below and discussed a bit further in chapter 6. Reflections on this term range from philosophies of history to cookbook instructions for market research.

 9 G. Lenski, *The Religious Factor*, Doubleday Anchor, New York, 1963, p. 331. Also see J. T. Flint, "Historical Role Analysis in the Study of Secularization: The Laity/Clergy Ratio in Norway: 1800–1950," *The Journal for the Scientific Study of Religion*, vol. 7, no. 2, Fall 1968, pp. 272–279.

10 Gerth and Mills, *Character and Social Structure*, p. 26 (paraphrased reduction).

11 See Michael Hill, *The Religious Order: A Study of Virtuoso Religion and its Legitimation in the Nineteenth-Century Church of England*, Heinemann Educational Books, London, 1973 (for a brief treatment and bibliography). For the Lutheran clerical parties, see chapter 2 below.

12 Joachim Wach, *Sociology of Religion*, University of Chicago Press, Chicago, 1944, pp. 175–188.

13 For examples, see Michael Hill, *A Sociology of Religion*, Basic Books, New York, 1973, chapters 2 and 3; J. Milton Yinger, *The Scientific Study of Religion*, McGraw-Hill, New York, 1970.

14 Cf. chapter 6 below, "Religious diversity and the ambiguity of secularity," for text and further citations from this abundant literature.

15 Flint, "Historical Role Analysis"; Robert Wuthnow (ed.), *The Religious Dimension: New Directions in Quantitative Research*, Academic Press, New York, 1979.

16 Sverre Steen, *Det Gamla Samfunn*, J. W. Cappelen, Oslo, 1957; Lennart Jorberg, "The Nordic Countries 1850–1914," in Carlo M. Cipolla (ed.), *The Fontana Economic History of Europe*, vol. IV, part 2, Collins/Fontana Books, London, 1970; Juul Bjerke, "Langtidslinjer i Norsk Økonomi 1865–1960," *Samfunnsøkonomiske Studier*, 16 Statistisk Sentralbyraa, Oslo, 1966. Depending on definitions of key terms there are, of course, variations in the dating of Norway's industrial take-off. My primary criterium is to large-scale concentrations of labor power in particular locations, and therefore most observers would locate this after 1900 if not 1890. This statement will be qualified in the text.

17 For useful general surveys of Norwegian history in English, see T. K. Derry, *A History of Modern Norway: 1814–1972*, Clarendon Press, Oxford, 1973. The standard work for many years has been Karen Larson, *A History of Norway*: New York, Princeton University Press for the American Scandinavian Foundation, 1950.

18 There is, of course, a very sizeable specialized literature on this parliamentary crisis period, but for the present purposes (in addition to Derry and Larson) cf. the work of Stein Rokkan – for example, "Norway: Numerical Democracy and Corporate Pluralism," in Robert A. Dahl (ed.), *Political Opposition in Western Democracies*, Yale University Press, New Haven and London, 1966, pp. 70–115.

2 Clerical generations

1 John T. Flint, "The Secularization of Norwegian Society," *Comparative Studies in Society and History*, vol. 4, no. 3, 1964, pp. 325–344, for a role-system analysis of the Norwegian religious order from tenth-century paganism to late-eighteenth-century Lutheran Rationalism. Also J. T. Flint, "State, Church and Laity in Norwegian Society: A Typological Study of Institutional Change," unpublished Doctoral Dissertation, University of Wisconsin, 1957, pp. 14–122.

2 My use of the terms "experiential," "ideological," "intellectual," "ritualistic," and "consequential" to distinguish styles of religiosity is drawn from Glock and Stark's effort to distinguish five dimensions of religiosity usable in contemporary survey research; see Charles Y. Glock and R. Stark, *Religion and Society in Tension*, Rand McNally, Chicago, 1965, chapter 2. While many critics find these dimensions simplistic, it is precisely this quality as well as their conventional and familiar features that recommend them to the historical sociologist, if not to all survey researchers. Joachim Wach's *Sociology of Religion*, University of Chicago Press, Chicago, 1944 contains an extensive elaboration and comparative historical treatment of similar though not identical conceptual devices.

3 Oluf Kolsrud, *Presteutdaningi i Noreg*, Scandinavian University Books, Oslo, 1962.

4 B. J. Hovde, *The Scandinavian Countries, 1720–1865*, vol. I, Cornell University Press, Ithaca, New York, 1948, pp. 93–103. See also Mary Fulbrook's more

extensive discussion of some varieties of Pietistic expression and organization in her recent *Piety and Politics: Religion and the Rise of Absolutism in England, Wurttemberg and Prussia*, Cambridge University Press, Cambridge, 1983. Also the article on Pietism by F. Ernest Stoeffler in Mircea Eliade (ed.), *The Encyclopedia of Religion*, MacMillan, New York, 1987, pp. 324–326. For a now very dated but still useful source see Paul Grunberg's article, "Pietism," in S. M. Jackson (ed.), *The New Schaff-Herzog Encyclopedia of Religious Knowledge*, Baker Book House, Grand Rapids, Michigan, 1953.

5 Dagfinn Mannsaaker, *Det Norske Presteskapet i det 19 Hundreaaret: Det Norske Samlaget*, Oslo, 1954, pp. 116–122. Sonja Pollan, "Prestetradisjon og Presterekruttering, 1720–1955," *Tidsskrift for Samfunnsforskning*, vol. 3, 1962, pp. 83–98. Einar Molland, *Fra Hans Nielsen Hauge til Eivind Bergrav*, revised editions, Gyldendal Norsk Forlag, Oslo, 1968.

6 A. Pontoppidan Thyssen, "Danmark," from a collection of papers on popular religious movements and society in Scandinavia between about 1750 and 1850, in *Nordisk Historiker Møtet*, vol. I, Historiallinen Arkisto 62 utgiven av Finske Historiska Samfundet, Helsingfors, 1967, pp. 7–38; see also Dagfinn Mannsaaker, "Norge," in *ibid.*, pp. 39–53.

7 Some critics of secularization studies have seen this assumption as the myth of an earlier supposed high level of religiosity. There is some evidence for pagan and Roman Catholic survivals as well as simple indifference and/or hostility to any clergy during earlier periods.

8 This assertion regarding the higher level of clerical control in Norway than Denmark is inferred from a reading of Thyssen and Mannsaaker in *Nordisk Historiker*.

9 Hans-Jørgen Dokka, *Fra Allmueskole til Folkeskole*, Universitetsforlaget, Oslo, 1967, and, in greater detail, Helge Dahl, *Norske Laererutdanning fra 1814 til i Dag*, Universitetsforlaget, Oslo, 1959.

10 Andreas Seierstad, *Kyrkjelegt Reformarbeid i Noreg i Nittande Hundreaaret*, Bibliotheca Norwegiae Sacrae, II, A/S Lunde & Co. Forlag, Bergen, 1923, pp. 7–8. This phenomenon would lend itself to rather extensive study simply on the basis of current secondary literature. To cite only two examples: Edward L. Cleary, *Crisis and Change: The Church in Latin America Today*, Orbis Books, Maryknoll, New York, 1985, a fascinating work on the interplay between liberation theology and base communities in Latin America, and Alan D. Gilbert's work on the political spin-offs of Methodist class meetings in the eighteenth century and later, particularly their unanticipated production of religious and political activists, *Religion and Society in Industrial England: Church, Chapel and Social Change, 1740–1914*, Longman, London and New York, 1976.

11 Herman Rugge, "Almendannelsen," in *Norsk Kulturhistorie*, vol. IV, J. W. Cappelens Forlag, Oslo, 1940, p. 420.

12 Flint, "Secularization," pp. 340–341.

13 John T. Flint, "Historical Role Analysis in the Study of Secularization: The Laity/Clergy Ratio in Norway: 1800–1950," *The Journal for the Scientific Study of Religion*, vol. 7, no. 2, 1968, pp. 272–279, for a more systematic discussion of the

rationale underlying historical role analysis in the study of religious change. The present monograph is a continuation of efforts begun there and in the 1964 article, "Secularization."

14 Dokka, *Fra Allmueskole*, p. 32.
15 Sverre Steen, *Det Gamla Samfunn*, J. W. Cappelen, Oslo, 1957.
16 Some contradictory evidence and alternative interpretations of these regional contrasts will be discussed in the concluding chapter, particularly the work done by Eilert Sundt.
17 Dokka, *Fra Allmueskole*, pp. 39–40.
18 Thyssen, "Danmark," p. 10.
19 Dokka, *Fra Allmueskole*, pp. 89–90.
20 Halvdan Koht, "Fra en Norsk Kirkestrid," *Symra*, vols. 3–4, 1907–8, pp. 59–70. Also, Molland, *Fra Hans Nielsen*, pp. 30–31.
21 Kolsrud, *Presteutdaningi*, p. 226.
22 Thyssen, "Danmark," p. 10; Flint, "State, Church and Laity," pp. 66–72.
23 Erik Pontoppidan's *Sannhet til Gudfryktighet* was reissued in a modern Norwegian translation from its first edition, Lutherstiftelsen, Oslo, 1964.
24 For example, see A. Christian Bang, *Hans Nielsen Hauge og Hans Samtid, Et tidsbillede fra omkring aar 1800*, J. W. Cappelens Forlag, Kristiania (Oslo), 1924, Fjerde Oplag.
25 Molland, *Fra Hans Nielsen*, pp. 26–27. A major gap in my present effort is a more extended treatment of Norwegian Grundtvigianism. This was prompted in part by the absence of any secondary literature providing reasonably "quantitative" descriptions of both the magnitude and social and geographical distribution of this party within the Norwegian clergy as well as (and more vitally) among school teachers after *c.* 1860. If this were to be pursued, the short monograph by Anders Skrøndal would be among the beginning points; see his *Grundtvigianismen i Noreg Kyrkje og Skule 1872–1890*, Bibliotheca Norwegiae Sacrae, SIII, A/S Lunde & Co. Forlag, Bergen, 1936. As to N. F. S. Grundtvig (1783–1872) – poet, scholar, theologian, Bishop, and, of most importance here, patron saint of the folk high school movement in Denmark and Norway – his importance to my work is obviously via his Norwegian followers, who often disagreed both with him and each other, issuing in diverse factions which probably diluted his impact considerably.
26 Flint, "State, Church and Laity," pp. 96–101; Kristian Valkner, "Landstads og Hauges Salmebøker, Tilblivelseshistorie og Hymnologisk Karakteristikk," Norvegia Sacra, *Aarbok til Kunnskap om den Norske Kirke i Fortid og Samtid*, Tolvte Aargang, Steenske Forlag, Oslo, 1932.
27 Flint, "State, Church and Laity," pp. 87–89, for a brief note on elite reading patterns in the eighteenth century.
28 Max Weber "Sociology of Religion," p. 507.
29 A more systematic comparative study of educational development and religious change would have to include close attention to the language of religious instruction *vis-à-vis* the vernacular, including dialect variations as a variable in the relationship.

30 Literature on the Hauge movement has been a continuing special field in Norwegian social and church history. For some English accounts, see Hovde, *Scandinavian Countries*, pp. 315–320; Joseph M. Shaw, *Pulpit under the Sky*, Augsburg Publishing House, Minneapolis, 1955; Flint, "State, Church and Laity," pp. 123–360.

31 For example see Patricia James' edition of *The Travel Diaries of T. R. Malthus*, Cambridge University Press, London, 1966, for an account of his travels in eastern Norway during 1799.

32 Hans Nielsen Hauge, *Autobiographical Writings*, trans. Joel M. Njus, Augsburg Publishing House, Minneapolis, 1954, pp. 98–99.

33 Mannsaaker, 1967, "Norge," in *Nordisk Historiker*, p. 43.

34 Dagfinn Mannsaaker, "Hans Nielsen Hauges Motstandarar," *Historisk Tidsskrift*, Oslo, vol. 41, 1962, p. 383.

35 Herman Rugge, "Almendannelsen," p. 420.

36 Dahl, *Norsk Laererutdanning*, pp. 92–94. Dahl provides the most comprehensive data on the social origins of students in those teacher seminaries which began to appear in the 1830s (see chapter 5 in the present text for a discussion of these). To my knowledge, comparable data are not available for ambulatory school teachers for earlier periods, except perhaps through local history research. I am assuming that they were similar to or lower than these seminarians in social origin. This is suggested by Dokka, *Fra Allmueskole*, p. 53 and Steen, *Gamla Samfunn*, p. 238.

37 Steen, *Gamla Samfunn*, p. 67.

38 Weber, "Sociology of Religion," pp. 468–518.

39 Mannsaaker, 1962, "Hauges Motstandarar," pp. 394–398.

40 *Ibid.*, p. 394.

41 Christian T. Jonassen, "The Protestant Ethic and the Spirit of Capitalism in Norway," *American Sociological Review*, vol. 12, 1947, pp. 676–686.

42 Flint, 1957, "State, Church and Laity," pp. 249–278, for a discussion of the Hauge movement as an incipient sect-type construct within the Weber/Troeltsch conceptual tradition.

43 Mannsaaker, *Norske Presteskapet*, p. 118.

44 Seierstad, *Kyrkjelegt Reformarbeid*, pp. 253–315.

45 *Ibid.*, pp. 316–335; Robert B. Cushman, "American Religious Societies in Norway," unpublished doctoral dissertation, Northwestern University, Evanston, Illinois, 1943.

46 Peter L. Berger, *The Sacred Canopy*, Doubleday Anchor, New York, 1969.

47 Gjerde, Jon, *From Peasants to Farmers: The Migration from Balestrand, Norway to the Upper Middle West*, Cambridge University Press, Cambridge, 1985. This superb micro-historical study of a West Country Norwegian district provides a quantitative insight into this process while seriously qualifying it as a generally valid statement.

48 Oddvar Bjørklund, *Marcus Thrane, En stridsmann for menneskerett og Fri Tanke*, Tiden Norsk Forlag, Oslo, 1951, pp. 181–188, for variations on tempo of growth and regional variations in magnitude; Edvard Bull, *Arbeiderklassen i Norsk Historie*, Tiden Norsk Forlag, Oslo, 1947, p. 62, for the 30,000 figure suggestion.

49 This oversimplifies the ideological interplay between the Thrane Movement, the church, and diverse religious impulses current at the time, but does point up an essential contrast.
50 Molland, *Fra Hans Nielsen*, 1968, pp. 30–31.
51 *Ibid.*, p. 126.

3 Organizational indicators

 1 Robert Currie, Alan Gilbert, and Lee Horsley, *Churches and Churchgoers: Patterns of Church Growth in the British Isles since 1700*, Clarendon Press, Oxford, 1977; Alan D. Gilbert, *Religion and Society in Industrial England: Church, Chapel and Social Change, 1740–1914*, Longman, London and New York, 1976.
 2 Ola Rudvin, *Indremisjonsselskapets Historie*, vol. I, *1868–1891*, vol. II, *1892–1968*, Lutherstiftelsens Forlag, Oslo, 1967 and 1970; John Nome, *Det Norske Misjonsselskaps Historie i Norsk Kirkeliv*, vols. I and II, Dreyers Grafiske Anstalt, Stavanger, 1943.
 3 My discussion of clergy/laity relationships, controversies, etc. in this chapter rests most notably on Molland, on Mannsaaker's *Norske Presteskapet*, on Nome, on Rudvin, and, to a lesser extent, on a scattering of other sources: e.g., Godvin Ousland, *En Kirkenhøvding: Professor Gisle Johnson som Teolog og Kirkemann*, Lutherstiftelsens Forlag, Oslo, 1950; Ulf Torgersen, *Church Independence and Doctrinal Purity*, Institute for Social Research, Oslo, 1966 (stenciled). Torgerson's immensely insightful and descriptively rich study focuses on the period after 1890; it has, however, been helpful at several points in the present work.
 4 See tables and discussion in chapter 5 below (esp. table 5.7).
 5 Mannsaaker, *Norske Presteskapet*, p. 121.
 6 Nome, *Norske Misjonsselskaps*, pp. 107–149.
 7 Molland, *Fra Hans Nielsen*, p. 42.
 8 Rudvin, *Indremisjonsselskapets*, vol. I, pp. 263–457.
 9 *Ibid.*, pp. 284–285.
10 *Ibid.*, vol. II, pp. 16–17.
11 *Ibid.*, p. 16.
12 Bernhard Eide, *Det Vestlandske Indremisjonsforbund gjennom 50 Aar*, Utgjeve av Det Vestlandske Indremisjonsforbund, Bergen, 1948.
13 Gabriel Øidne, "Litt om Motsetninga Mellom Austlandet og Vestlandet," *Syn og Segn*, vol. 63, no. 3, 1957, pp. 97–114.
14 *Norges Officielle Statistikk*, Raekke III, No. 278, Folketaellingen 1 januar 1891. Folkemaengde fordelt efter . . . trosbekjendelse. (This report includes several other population attributes in addition to religious identities of those outside the state church.)
15 Molland, *Fra Hans Nielsen*, pp. 106–107.
16 *Ibid.*, pp. 108–109.
17 Seierstad, *Kyrkjelegt Reformarbeid*, pp. 320–324.
18 Nome, *Norske Misjonsselskaps*, vol. II, p. 55.

19 *Ibid.* For a particularly sustained and bitter controversy, however, see pp. 258–271, vol. I.
20 *Ibid.*, vol. I, pp. 69–95.
21 Molland, *Fra Hans Nielsen*, pp. 46–47; Stein Rokkan, "Geography, Religion and Social Class: Cross Cutting Cleavages in Norwegian Politics," in S. M. Lipset and S. Rokkan (eds.), *Party Systems and Voter Alignments*, The Free Press, New York, 1967, pp. 363–403.
22 Molland, *Fra Hans Nielsen*, p. 123.

4   Elite literacy

1 Mannsaaker, *Norske Presteskapet*, pp. 136–216. This remains, in my judgment, the most systematic effort to construct a profile of social stratification in nineteenth-century Norwegian society available in the literature. Several others have contributed to this problem (e.g., Semmingsen, Steen, Skappel) and will be noted as used in the present and following chapter. For a sociological overview with an emphasis upon modern Norwegian society, see Vilhelm Aubert, "Stratification," in Natalie Rogoff Ramsøy (ed.) *Norwegian Society*, Universitetsforlaget, Oslo, 1968, pp. 108–157.
2 The historical–ecological work of Stein Rokkan and his co-workers is fundamental to any assessment of political economic processes, particularly in late-nineteenth-century Norwegian society, and will be discussed briefly later. Among his several relevant publications, see Stein Rokkan, "Norway: Numerical Democracy and Corporate Pluralism," in Robert A. Dahl (ed.), *Political Opposition in Western Democracies*, Yale University Press, New Haven and London, 1966, pp. 70–115; Stein Rokkan and Henry Valen, "Regional Contrasts in Norwegian Politics," in E. Allardt and Y. Littunen (eds.), *Cleavages, Ideologies and Party Systems: Contributions to Comparative Political Sociology*, Transactions of the Westermarck Society, Helsinki, 1964, pp. 162–238.
3 Dokka, *Fra Allmueskole*, p. 25. A more refined picture of the regional distribution of (rural) children experiencing private instruction may be gained from the several reports to the Department of Church and Education cited in the bibliography; for the pre-1860 period see those for 1837 and 1853, from which Dokka draws his national aggregate figures.
4 Flint, "State, Church and Laity," pp. 77–105, particularly, "Some Dimensions of the Enlightenment in the Norwegian Religious Order."
5 Vilhelm Aubert *et al.*, "Akademikere i Norsk Samfunnsstruktur 1800–1950," *Tidsskrift for Samfunnsforkning*, Aargang, no. 4, December 1960, pp. 185–204. Of related interest, see Ulf Torgersen, *The Market for Professional Manpower in Norway*, Institute for Social Research, Oslo, 1967 (stenciled); Henrik Palmstrøm, "Om en befolkningsgruppes utvikling gjennom de siste 100 aar. Statistiske studies vedrørende norske akademikere," *Statsøkonomisk Tidsskrift*, 1935 (Oslo), pp. 161–370.
6 Tore Lindbekk, "Filologer og realister i norsk samfunnsstruktur," *Tidsskrift for Samfunnsforskning*, 2 Aargang, no. 2, June 1961, pp. 117–132.
7 *Ibid.*, Table 2, p. 121.

8 *Historisk Statistikk, 1968*, Statistisk Sentralbyraa, Oslo, 1969, p. 687, table 1, p. 337.

9 Ingrid Semmingsen, "The Dissolution of Estate Society in Norway," *Scandinavian Economic History Review*, vol. 2, 1954, p. 194.

10 Harold L. Tveteraas, *Norske Tidsskrifter, Bibliografi over periodiske skrifter i Norge Inntil 1920*, Universitetsbiblioteket, Oslo, 1940; see particularly pp. v–xv, and the summary overview table, p. vii.

11 Ola Rudvin, *Den Kristelige Presse i Norge*, Lutherstiftelsens Forlag, Oslo, 1947, pp. 67–69.

12 Tveteraas, *Norske Tidsskrifter*, p. vi.

13 Per Maurseth, "Naeringslivet," in Vilhelm Aubert *et al.*, *Det Norske Samfunn: En Sosiologisk Beskrivelse*, Institutet for Sosiologi, Oslo, 1966 (stenciled; see its chapter 3, table 2 [no continuous pagination]). Svennik Høyer, "The Political Economy of the Norwegian Press," *Scandinavian Political Studies*, vol. 3, 1968, pp. 85–143.

14 Harold Beyer, *A History of Norwegian Literature*, trans. and ed. Einar Haugen, New York University Press, New York, 1966, pp. 167–250. For a standard English survey more pointed to the present concern, Molland, *Fra Hans Nielsen*, pp. 53–62.

15 Molland, *Fra Hans Nielsen*, pp. 35–36.

16 *Ibid.*, p. 34.

17 Mannsaaker, *Norske Presteskapet*, pp. 97–98.

18 Ulf Torgersen, *Church Independence*, pp. 2.1.4; 4.5.11.

19 Mannsaaker, *Norske Presteskapet*, p. 201, table 23.

20 Aubert *et al.*, "Akademikere"; Lindbekk, "Filologer."

21 Mannsaaker, *Norske Presteskapet*, pp. 217–235, particularly his table 30, "Marriage between Pastors and Pastors Wives from Different Social Strata," which provides a matrix of his four strata showing cross-strata marriage aggregated for periods 1801–1860 and then 1861–1910.

22 Thomas Mathiesen and Otto Hauglin, "Religion," in Rogoff Ramsøy (ed.), *Norwegian Society*, pp. 245–246. Their analysis of the occupational composition of Norwegian Dissenters in the 1960 census does *not* support this idea; e.g., see p. 246.

23 Einar Molland, *Church Life in Norway 1800–1950*, trans. Harris Kaasa, first edition of *Fra Hans Nielsen Hauge til Eivind Bergrav*, second edn published by Augsburg Publishing House, Minneapolis, 1957, p. 41. See also Harris Kaasa, "Ibsen and the Theologians," *Scandinavian Studies*, vol. 43, no. 4, 1971, pp. 356–384.

24 Carl Fr. Wisløff, *Politikk og Kristendom*, en studie omkring oppropet "Til Christendommens Venner i vort Land" (January 1883), A. S. Lunde & Co's Forlag, Bergen, 1961.

5 Mass educational experience

1 Dokka, *Fra Allmueskole*; Dahl, *Norske Laererutdanning*; scattered reference is made to both throughout this section.

2 Dokka, *Fra Allmueskole*, p. 109; Dahl, *Norske Laererutdanning*, p. 105.

3 Dokka, *Fra Allmueskole*, pp. 207–210; his tables and text here first made me aware

of these resources. *Norges Officielle Statistikk*, Aeldre Raekke A no. 1, Beretning om Alumneskolevaesenets Tilstand i Kongeriget Norges Landdistrikt aaren 1861 & 1873; for 1891 see N.O.S., Raekke III, no. 212, Folkeskolesvaesenets tilstand i rigets landdistrikter. The administrative units utilized by the Ministry of Church and Education in its statistical description of rural school conditions changed rather drastically between 1861 and 1873. Information for the former years was published according to diocese and deaneries, while the latter year used diocese and provinces. The importance of this problem is rather minimized by the fact that my main regional contrast has usually been between East Country and West Country dioceses: that is, Oslo and Hamar in the east and Agder and Bergen to the west. Hamar diocese was formed in 1864 when Oppland and Hedmark provinces were separated from the Oslo diocese. Also, in 1863 Bamble and lower Telemark deaneries were shifted from Oslo to Agder diocese for administrative purposes. Finally, as I have noted at one point in the text, the province of Møre and Romsdal was divided between Bergen (Møre) and Trondhjem (Romsdal) dioceses. Where such changes have had some bearing on the main line of my argument I have dealt with it in the text. The most debatable problems and procedures came in allocating the several deaneries within Oslo diocese between the provinces of Akershus, Østfold, and Buskerud. Again, since variations within the Oslo diocese were not of central concern to me I have not reported the procedures used in making these decisions.

4 Dokka, *Fra Allmueskole*, pp. 212–213.
5 *Norges Officielle Statistikk*, school reports for 1861 and 1873.
6 Dahl, *Norske Laererutdanning*, pp. 87–89.
7 *Historisk Statistikk, 1969*, Statistisk Sentralbyraa, *1968*, p. 603, table 330.
8 These data on the shift in teacher's income from payment in kind to cash might be interpreted as a partial indicator of the timing and tempo of regional variations in the monetization of the rural economy.
9 Tveteraas, *Norske Tideskrifter*, p. xiv, Gruppe P.; see also Dokka, *Fra Allmueskole*, pp. 237–238 for the unreliable and shaky support of teachers for these journals.
10 *Historisk Statistikk*, p. 603, table 330.
11 The possible implications of these ratio contrasts will be considered below. There is some evidence to indicate that the actual number of school days each year did not increase significantly until after 1891.
12 Dokka, *Fra Allmueskole*, pp. 56–57, tables 2 and 3.
13 Odd Ramsfjell, *Kristendomsfaget i Folkeskolen: En historisk oversikt og en undersøkning*, Magister Grad Avhandling, Oslo, 1960.
14 Dokka, *Fra Allmueskole*, p. 247 (paraphrase translation).
15 *Ibid.*, p. 249 (paraphrase translation).
16 *Ibid.*, p. 248.
17 Ramsfjell, *Kristendomsfaget*; compare his class timetables for 1864 (table 1, p. 5) and 1889 (table 3, p. 8). There appear to be some significant diocesan variations in 1864: i.e., more time devoted to religious education in the West Country than the East, etc.

18 *Norges Officielle Statistikk*, Aeldre Raekke, table no. 28, Folkemaengde fordelt efter Fødesteder C no. 1, Folketaellingen i Norge, January 1876.
19 Semmingsen, "Dissolution of Estate Society," p. 181; Edvard Bull, *Arbeiderklassen i Norsk Historie*, Tiden Norsk Forlag, Oslo, 1947, pp. 57–58.
20 Simen Skappel, "Om Husmandsvaesenet i Norge," in *Skrifter utgitt av Videnskapsselskapet i Kristiania*, II Historisk-Filosofisk Klasse 2 Bind, Kristiania i Kommission Hos Jacob Dybwad, 1922, p. 177.
21 Steen, *Gamla Samfunn*, pp. 55–60.
22 Folketaellingen i Norge, January 1876, C no. 1, *Norges Officielle Statistikk*, Aeldre Raekke, 1876; table no. 21, "Mandspersoner over 15 Aar med enkelte og kombinerede Livsstillinger."
23 *Norges Officielle Statistikk*, Raekke III, Folketaellinger 1, January 1891, table no. 7.
24 Rigmor Fremannslund, "Farm Community and Neighbourhood Community," *Scandinavian Economic History Review*, vol. 4, 1956, p. 64.
25 Pontoppidan, *Sannhet*, pp. 43–50.
26 The relationship between the Thrane Movement and lay activists, Haugean particularly, was not totally negative for qualifications on this. See Flint, "State, Church and Laity," and also Rudvin, *Indremisjons*, vol. I, pp. 150–161.
27 Torgersen, *Church Independence*, makes a comparable contrast for a later period.
28 Semmingsen, "Dissolution of Estate Society," p. 198.
29 Dahl, *Norske Laererutdanning*, pp. 92–94; Dokka, *Fra Allmueskole*, p. 234.
30 Mannsaaker, *Norske Presteskapet*, p. 174, table 20.
31 *Ibid.*, p. 169, table 19.
32 Theodor Geiger, *Den Danske Intelligens Fra Reformationen til Nutiden: En studie en empirisk Kultursociologi*. Universitetsforlaget i Aarhus, Ejnar Munksgaard, Copenhagen, 1949, pp. 138–151.
33 Weber, "Sociology of Religion," pp. 468–517; for Scandinavia up to 1865, see Hovde, *Scandinavian Countries*, pp. 303–347.
34 Bang, *Hans Nielsen Hauge*; H. G. Heggtveit, *Den Norske Kirke i det Nittende Aaerhundrede*, 3 vols., Kra., Oslo, 1912–1920.
35 It is probable that several LF agents also worked for regional associations, at least during those seasons when they were not retained by LF.
36 Rudvin, *Indremisjons*, pp. 458–480.
37 *Ibid.*, pp. 480–484.
38 The historical–ecological archive at the University of Bergen will soon include more adequate data on local religious associations, thereby expanding existing holdings on language associations, local temperance societies, and other political associations.
39 Staale Dyrvik, "Overgangen til Sjølveige i Norge, Nokre nye data for 1700-talet," *Historisk Tidsskrift*, vol. 56, no. 1, 1977, pp. 1–18. This contains, among other items, tax data at something like the deanery level (actually, tax districts which seem to correspond to them) for the period 1661–1801.
40 Eilert Sundt, *Om Saedelighedstilstanden i Norge*, vols. I and II, Pax Forlag, Oslo, 1968 (first edition, 1857), pp. 39–40.

41 There are some variations among scholars regarding the total size and provincial distribution of the Thrane Movement, but for present purposes these are not particularly vital.

42 John T. Flint, "The Church in Relation to Family Life," in T. D. Eliot and Arthur Hillman (eds.), *Norway's Families*, University of Pennsylvania Press, Philadelphia, 1960, pp. 387–406. Also, on regional variations in church attendance patterns in the mid 1950s, see Gunnar Spilling, "Resultater av Kirketelling og Opinionsundersøkerser," *Kirke og Kultar*, vol. 62, 1957, pp. 385–399.

43 Løiten (1881), Nordre Odalen (1885–87), Tynset (1889); the following parishes are not reported by Rudvin at any point at least up to 1894: Hof, Vaaler, Aamodt, Rendal, Tolgen, Lille Elvdalen, Kvikne.

44 Rudvin, *Indremisjons*, p. 184; Tynset was also the only reported affiliate in Upper Østerdalen – reported in 1889.

45 Sundt, *Om Saedelighedstilstanden*, table 22, "Skolerne of Saedeligheden," p. 308.

46 It is probable that local-level historical studies in Europe and the United States have become sufficiently numerous to merit a bibliographic essay, if several such have not already appeared unnoticed by me. However, so far as I know, those including local-level interaction between pastors or priests and school teachers with a laity have not. Barnett Singer's *Village Notables in Nineteenth-Century France: Priests, Mayors, Schoolmasters*, State University of New York Press, Albany, 1983, contains relevant material. Hans Try's near classic local history study, *Gardsskipnad og Bondenaering: Sørlandsk jordbruk paa 1800-talet* [Farm organization and Southland Farm Economy: Agriculture in the 1800s], Universitetsforlaget, Oslo, 1969, I rather assume could be expanded to include educational and religious dimensions. I assume he would be the person to do so, if interested. This centers on a single commune, Søgne, in Vest-Agder. In so far as Jon Gjerde's work relates to these issues in *From Peasants to Farmers*, the focus tends to be on the American scene. It is my impression that most local history scholars in Norway of a "cliometric" persuasion are likely to limit their descriptions to topics (like Try's and Gjerde's) for which reasonably reliable official statistics (tax records, etc.) are available. I have not really kept up with the work of Staale Dyrvik and his associates and so may have missed relevant research publications.

6 Religious diversity

1 Flint, "Historical Role Analysis"; see chapter 1 above for the rationale underlying this ratio.

2 Mannsaaker, *Norske Presteskapet*, p. 72.

3 By 1952 the ratio of official parish clergy to total population was about 1/3,550. It is important to note that this does *not* include trained theologians in non-parish posts or unordained religious functionaries within voluntary organizations, etc.

4 Peter L. Berger, *The Sacred Canopy*, Doubleday Anchor, New York, 1967.

5 See, Hill, *Sociology of Religion*; Yinger, *Scientific Study of Religion*; and Brian Wilson, *Religious Sects*, McGraw-Hill, New York, 1970.

6 Wach, *Sociology of Religion*, pp. 175–188.

7 Michael Hill, *The Religious Order: A Study of Virtuoso Religion and its Legitimation in the Nineteenth-Century Church of England*, Heinemann Educational Books, London, 1973; John T. Flint, "Conceptual Translations in Comparative Study," in *Comparative Studies in Society and History*, vol. 18, no. 4, October 1976, pp. 502–516.

8 Werner Stark, *The Sociology of Religion: A Study of Christendom*, Fordham University Press, New York, vol. II, 1967; also see my review essay of his first three volumes in *Journal of the American Academy of Religion*, vol. 40, no. 1, March 1972, pp. 110–116.

9 Phillip E. Hammond, "The Migrating Sect: An Illustration from Early Norwegian Immigration," *Social Forces*, vol. 41, no. 3, March 1963, pp. 275–283; also, Flint, "Conceptual Translations," pp. 505–509; Nicholas Tavuchis, *Pastors and Immigrants*, Nijhoff, The Hague, 1963.

10 Hovde, *Scandinavian Countries*, p. 311.

11 Currie *et al.*, *Churches and Churchgoers*. Their focus is upon fluctuations in patterns of church membership and attendance in major English religious groups, not on secularization as such. Among the more acute critics of the concept see David Martin, *The Religious and the Secular*, Schocken Books, New York, 1969.

12 Berger, *The Sacred Canopy*, p. 107.

13 Molland, *Fra Hans Nielsen*, p. 39.

14 *Ibid.*, pp. 29–31, 48–52. There is a sizeable literature on Norwegian Grundtvigianism, but much of it appears to be intellectual–historical and biographical accounts of the folk high school movement, little of which provides much sense of just how intensive and extensive its actual distribution was.

15 Oddvar Bjørklund, *Marcus Thrane*; Aksel Zachariassen, *Fra Marcus Thrane til Martin Tranmael*, Arbeidernes Opplysningsforbund, Oslo, 1962. See also Øidne, "Litt om Motsetninga."

16 Alf Kaartvedt, *Kampen mot Parlamentarisme 1880–1884*, 2 udgave, Universitetsforlaget, Bergen-Oslo-Tromsø, 1967; Carl Fr. Wisløff, *Politikk og Kristendom*; Ulf Torgersen, "The Formation of Parties in Norway: The Problem of Right–Left Differences," *Scandinavian Political Studies*, vol. 2, 1967, pp. 43–68.

17 Stein Rokkan, "Geography, Religion and Social Class: Crosscutting Cleavages in Norwegian Politics," in S. M. Lipset and S. Rokkan (eds.), *Party Systems and Voter Alignments*, The Free Press, New York, 1967, pp. 363–403; Øidne, "Litt om Motsetninga"; Frank H. Aarebrot, "Regional Differences in Political Mobilization in Norway," *International Journal of Politics*, Spring–Summer 1974, pp. 91–94. Also, Aarebrot and D. W. Urwin, "The Politics of Cultural Dissent: Religion, Language and Demonstrative Effects in Norway," *Scandinavian Political Studies*, vol. 2, N.S., no. 2, 1979, pp. 75–98.

18 Glock and Stark, *Religion and Society*, p. 224; Flint, "Historical Role Analysis," p. 274.

19 Rokkan, "Geography, Religion," pp. 374–375.

20 Wisløff, *Politikk*. A copy of that manifesto is to be found in an appendix here. Wisløff's very helpful work is significantly organized around that statement. Indeed his subtitle, not included in my citation, makes that focus explicit.

21 Kaartvedt, *Kampen*, and Torgersen, *Formation of Parties*, devote particular attention to the timing, tempo, and regional distribution of these associations.
22 Rokkan and Valen, *Regional Contrasts*, p. 168.
23 Dokka, *Fra Allmueskole*, pp. 238–239.
24 Wisløff, *Politikk*, pp. 185–186, 167–169.
25 Lawrence Stone, "Literacy and Education in England: 1640–1900," *Past and Present*, no. 42, February 1969, p. 81.
26 Torgersen, *Church Independence and Doctrinal Purity*. This volume remains the single most helpful, insightful, social-scientifically oriented account of the thirty-year period after 1891 dealing with themes closely related to those which have concerned me in this essay. Unfortunately, it remains in stenciled form. Also see J. T. Flint, "The Church in Relation to Family Life," in T. D. Eliot and Arthur Hillman (eds.), *Norway's Families*, University of Pennsylvania Press, Philadelphia, 1960, pp. 387–406.

Bibliography

Reports from Norway's Central Statistical Bureau (Norges Officielle Statistikk) (N.O.S.)

Fortegnelse over Norges Officielle Statistikk 1828–1950
Statistiske Tabeller vedkommende Undervisningsvaesenets Tilstand i Norge ved Udgangen af Aaret, 1837
Statistiske Tabeller vedkommende Undervisningsvaesenets Tilstand i Norge i 1853
Beretning om Almueskolevaesenets Tilstand i Kongeriget Norges Landdistrikt for Aarene, 1861 and 1873, Aeldre Raekke, A no. 1
Folketaellingen i Norge, January 1876, C No. 1, N.O.S. Aeldre Raekke
Beretning om Almueskolevaesenets Tilstand, 1880, Ny Raekke
Folkeskolevaesenets tilstand i Rigets landdistriker, 1891, Raekke, III, no. 212
Folketaellingen i Kongeriget Norge, 1 January 1891, Tredie Raekke, nos. 236 and 278
Utvandringsstatistikk, 1921, Raekke VII, no. 25
Historisk Statistikk, 1968, Statistisk Sentralbyraa, Oslo, 1969

Secondary sources

Aarebrot, Frank H., "Regional Differences in Political Mobilization in Norway: Local Infrastructure Development, Political Polarization, and Suffrage Extension, 1868–1897," *International Journal of Politics*, vol. 4, no. 1–2, Spring/Summer 1974, pp. 91–140.

Aarebrot, Frank H. and Derek W. Urwin, "The Politics of Cultural Dissent: Religion, Language and Demonstrative Effects in Norway," *Scandinavian Political Studies*, vol. 2, N.S., no. 2, 1979, pp. 75–98.

Aarflot, Andreas, *Norske Kirkehistorie* Lutherstiftelsen, Oslo, 1967.

Altick, Richard D., *The English Common Reader: A Social History of the Mass Reading Public 1800–1900*, University of Chicago Press, Chicago, 1957.

Anderson, C. A. and Mary Jean Bowman (eds.), *Education and Economic Development*, Aldine, Chicago, 1963.

Aubert, Vilhelm, Ulf Torgersen, Karl Tangen, Tore Lindbekk, and Sonja Pollan, "Akademikere i norsk Samfunnsstruktur 1800–1950," *Tidsskrift for Samfunnsforskning*, 1 Aargang, no. 4, December 1960, pp. 185–204.

"Stratification," in Natalie Rogoff (Ramsøy (ed.), *Norwegian Society*, Universitetsforlaget, Oslo, 1968, pp. 108–157.

Aubert, Vilhelm, Ulf Torgersen, Karl Tangen, Tore Lindbekk, Sonja Pollan, and Francesco Kjellberg, *The Professions in Norwegian Social Structure 1720–1955*, Institute for Social Research, Oslo, vols. I and II, 1961 [no pagination].

Bang, A. Christian, *Hans Nielsen Hauge og Hans Samtid, El Tidsbillede fra omkring aar 1800*, J. W. Cappelens Forlag, Kristiania (Oslo), 1924, Fjerde Oplag.

Berger, Peter L., *The Sacred Canopy*, Doubleday Anchor, New York, 1969.

Beyer, Harold, *A History of Norwegian Literature*, trans. and ed. Einar Haugen, New York University Press, New York, 1956.

Bjerke, Juul, *Langtidslinjer i Norsk Økonomi 1865–1960*, Samfunnsøkonomiske Studier, 16, Statistisk Sentralbyraa, Oslo, 1966.

Bjørklund, Oddvar, *Marcus Thrane: En stridsmann for menneskerett og Fri Tanke*, Tiden Norsk Forlag, Oslo, 1951.

Bull, Edvard, *Arbeiderklassen i Norsk Historie*, Tiden Norsk Forlag, Oslo, 1947.

Cipolla, Carlo, M., *Literacy and Development in the West*, Penguin Books, Baltimore, Maryland, 1969.

Cleary, Edward L., O.P., *Crisis and Change: The Church in Latin America Today*, Orbis Books, Maryknoll, New York, 1985.

Coleman, James S. (ed.), *Education and Political Development*, Princeton University Press, Princeton, 1965.

Currie, Robert, Alan Gilbert, and Lee Horsley, *Churches and Churchgoers: Patterns of Church Growth in the British Isles Since 1700*, Clarendon Press, Oxford, 1977.

Dahl, Helge, *Norske Laererutdanning fra 1814 til i Dag*, Universitetsforlaget, Oslo, 1959.

Derry, T. K., *A History of Modern Norway: 1814–1972*, Clarendon Press, Oxford, 1973.

Dobbelaere, Karel, "Secularization: A Multi-Dimensional Concept," *Current Sociology*, vol. 29, no. 2, Summer 1981, pp. 1–215.

Dokka, Hans Jørgen, *Fra Allmueskole til Folkeskole*, Universitetsforlaget, Oslo, 1967.

Dore, R. P., *Education in Tokugawa Japan*, University of California Press, Berkeley, 1965.

Drake, Michael, *Population and Society in Norway: 1735–1865*, Cambridge University Press, Cambridge, 1969.

Drake, Michael (ed.), *Applied Historical Studies: An Introductory Reader*, Methuen and Company Ltd., London, 1973.

Dyrvik, Staale, *Den Lange Fredstiden 1720–1784,* vol. VIII of *Norges Historie* (ed. Knut Mykland), J. W. Cappelens Forlag, Oslo 1977.

   "Overgangen til Sjølveige i Norge, Nokre nye data for 1700-talet," *Historisk Tidsskrift*, vol. 56, no. 1, 1977, pp. 1–18.

Eide, Bernhard, *Det Vestlandske Indremisjonsforbund gjennom 50 Aar*, Utgjeve av Det Vestlandske Indremisjonsforbund, Bergen, 1948.

Flint, John T., "State, Church and Laity in Norwegian Society: A Typological Study of Institutional Change," unpublished Doctoral Dissertation, University of Wisconsin, 1957.

   "The Church in Relation to Family Life," in T. D. Eliot and Arthur Hillman (eds.), *Norway's Families*, University of Pennsylvania Press, Philadelphia, 1960, pp. 387–406.

"The Secularization of Norwegian Society," *Comparative Studies in Society and History*, vol. 4, no. 3, 1964, pp. 325–344.

"A Handbook for Historical Sociologists," *Comparative Studies in Society and History*, vol. 10, no. 4, July 1968, pp. 492–509.

"Historical Role Analysis in the Study of Secularization: The Laity/Clergy Ratio in Norway: 1800–1950," *The Journal for the Scientific Study of Religion*, vol. 7, no. 2, Fall 1968, pp. 272–279.

"Stark's *Sociology of Religion*: A Review Essay" (first three volumes), *Journal of the American Academy of Religion*, vol. 40, no. 1, March 1972, pp. 110–116.

"Conceptual Translations in Comparative Study," *Comparative Studies in Society and History*, vol. 18, no. 4, October 1976, pp. 502–516.

Foster, Philip J., "Education and Social Differentiation in Less-Developed Countries," *Comparative Education Review*, vol. 21, nos. 2 and 3, 1977 (special issue), pp. 211–229.

Freimannslund, Rigmor, "Farm Community and Neighborhood Community," *Scandinavian Economic History Review*, vol. 4, 1956, pp. 62–81.

Fuglum, Per, *Norge i Støpeskjeen 1884–1920*, vol. XII of *Norges Historie* (ed. Knut Mykland), J. W. Cappelens Forlag, Oslo, 1978.

Fulbrook, Mary, *Piety and Politics: Religion and the Rise of Absolutism in England, Wurttemberg and Prussia*, Cambridge University Press, Cambridge, 1983.

Geiger, Theodor, *Den Danske Intelligens Fra Reformationen til Nutiden: En studie i empirisk kultursociologi*, Universitetsforlaget i Aarhus, Ejnar Munksgaard, Copenhagen, 1949.

Gerth, Hans and C. Wright Mills, *Character and Social Structure*, Harcourt, Brace and World, New York, 1953.

Gilbert, Alan D., *Religion and Society in Industrial England: Church, Chapel and Social Change: 1740–1914*, Longman, London and New York, 1976.

Gjerde, Jon, *From Peasants to Farmers: The Migration from Balestrand, Norway to the Upper Middle West*, Cambridge University Press, Cambridge, 1985.

Glock, Charles Y., and Rodney Stark, *Religion and Society in Tension*, Rand McNally, Chicago, 1965.

Goody, Jack (ed.), *Literacy in Traditional Societies*, Cambridge University Press, Cambridge, 1968.

Graff, Harvey J., *The Literacy Myth: Literacy and Social Structure in the 19th Century City*, Academic Press, New York, 1979.

Hammond, Peter C., *The Parson and the Victorian Parish*, Hodder and Stoughton, London, 1977.

Hammond, Phillip E., "The Migrating Sect: An Illustration from Early Norwegian Immigration," *Social Forces*, vol. 41, no. 3, March 1963, pp. 275–283.

Hansteen, Carsten, *Av Det Norske Kristenlivs Psykologi*, Bibliotheca Norvegiae Sacrae, I, 1922 B, A. S. Lunde and Company, Bergen, 1922.

Harbison, Frederick, and Charles A. Myers, *Education, Manpower, and Economic Growth*, McGraw-Hill, New York, 1964.

Hauge, Hans Nielsen, *Autobiographical Writings*, trans. Joal M. Njus, Augsburg Publishing House, Minneapolis, 1954.

Heffermehl, A. V., *Folkeundervisningen i Norge Indtil Omrking Aar 1700*, Grøndahl and Søns Forlag, Christiania, 1913.

Heggtveit, H. G., *Den Norske Kirke i det Nittende Aarhundrede*, 3 vols., Kra, Oslo, 1912–1920.

Higley, John, G. Lowell Field, and Knut Grøholt, *Elite Structure and Ideology: A Theory with Applications to Norway*, Universitetsforlaget, Oslo, 1976.

Hill, Michael, *A Sociology of Religion*, Basic Books, Inc., New York, 1973.
  The Religious Order: A Study of Virtuoso Religion and Its Legitimation in the Nineteenth Century Church of England, Heinemann Educational Books, London, 1973.

Hobsbawm, E. J. and Joan W. Scott, "Political Shoemakers," *Past and Present*, no. 89, November 1980, pp.86–114.

Hoigaard, Einar and Hermann Ruge, *Den Norske Skoles Historie: En Oversikt*, J. W. Cappelen, Oslo, 1963.

Hopkins, Terence and Immanuel Wallerstein, "Research Proposal: Patterns of Development of the Modern World-System," *Review*, vol. 1, no. 2, Fall 1977, pp. 111–145.

Houston, R. A., *Scottish Literacy and the Scottish Identity: Illiteracy and Society in Scotland and Northern England, 1600–1800*, Cambridge University Press, Cambridge, 1985.

Hovde, B. J., *The Scandinavian Countries, 1720–1865*, vol. I, Cornell University Press, Ithaca, New York, 1948, pp. 93–103.

Høyer, Svennik, "The Political Economy of the Norwegian Press," *Scandinavian Political Studies*, vol. 3, 1968, pp. 85–143.

James, Patricia (ed.), *The Travel Diaries of T. R. Malthus*, Cambridge University Press, London, 1966.

Jansen, T. D., "Elementary Teacher Education in Norway: A Descriptive Historical Study," unpublished M. A. Thesis, U.C.L.A., September 1957, pp. 1–141.

Jensen, Arne S., "Rural Schools in Norway," Ph.D. thesis, University of Washington, 1928.

Jonassen, Christian T., "The Protestant Ethic and the Spirit of Capitalism in Norway," *American Sociological Review*, vol. 12, 1947, pp. 676–686.

Jorberg, Lennart, "The Nordic Countries 1850–1914," in *The Fontana Economic History of Europe*, vol. IV, part 2, ed. Carlo M. Cipolla, Collins/Fontana Books, London, 1970.

Kaartvedt, Alf, *Kampen mot Parlamentarisme 1880–1884: Den konservative politikken under vetostriden*, second edition, Universitetsforlaget, Bergen–Oslo–Tromsø, 1967.

Karabel, Jerome and A. H. Halsey (eds.), *Power and Ideology in Education*, Oxford University Press, New York, 1977.

Koht, Halvdan, "Fra en Norsk Kirkestrid," *Symra*, vol. 3–4, 1907–1908, pp. 59–70.

Kolsrud, Oluf, *Presteutdaningi i Noreg*, Scandinavian University Books, Oslo, 1962.

Lenski, G., *The Religious Factor*, Doubleday Anchor, New York, 1963.

Lindbekk, Tore, "Filologer og realister i norsk samfunnsstruktur," *Tidsskrift for Samfunnsforskning*, 2 Aargang, no. 2, June 1961, pp. 117–132.

Linz, Juan J. and Amando De Miguel, "Within-Nation Differences and Comparisons:

The Eight Spains," in Richard L. Merritt and Stein Rokkan (eds.), *Comparing Nations: The Use of Quantitative Data in Cross-National Research*, Yale University Press, New Haven and London, 1966, pp. 267–319.

Lockridge, Kenneth A., *Literacy in Colonial New England: An Enquiry into the Social Context of Literacy in Early Modern Life*, W. W. Norton, New York, 1974.

Mannsaaker, Dagfinn, *Det Norske Presteskapet i det 19 Hundreaaret*, Det Norske Samlaget, Oslo, 1954, pp. 116–122.

"Hans Nielsen Hauges Motstandarar," *Historisk Tidsskrift* (Oslo), vol. 41, 1962, p. 383.

"Norge," in *Nordisk Historiker Møtet*, vol. I, Historiallinen Arkisto 62 utgiven av Finske Historiska Samfundet, Helsinki, 1967, pp. 39–53.

Martin, David, *The Religious and the Secular*, Schocken Books, New York, 1969.

A General Theory of Secularization, Harper Colophon Books, New York, 1978.

Mathiesen, Thomas and Otto Haughlin, "Religion," in Natalie Rogoff Ramsøy (ed.), *Norwegian Society*, Universitetsforlaget, Oslo, 1968, pp. 226–259.

Maurseth, Per, "Naeringsliv," in Vilhelm Aubert, *et al.*, *Det Norske Samfunn: En Sosiologisk Beskrivelse*, Institutet for Sosiologi, Oslo, 1966, ch. 3.

Moe, Thorvald, *Demographic Developments and Economic Growth in Norway 1740–1940*, Arno Press, New York, 1977.

Molland, Einar, *Fra Hans Nielsen Hauge til Eivind Bergrav*, revised, Gyldendal Norsk Forlag, Oslo, 1968.

Church Life in Norway 1800–1950, trans. Harris Kaasa, first edition of *Fra Hans Nielsen Hauge til Eivind Bergrav*, second edn published by Augsburg Publishing House, Minneapolis, 1957.

Musgrave, P. W. (ed.), *Sociology, History and Education*, London: Methuen & Co., 1970.

Mykland, Knut, *Kampen om Norge 1784–1814*, vol. IX of *Norges Historie* (ed. Knut Mykland), J. W. Cappelens Forlag, Oslo, 1977.

Noah, H. J. and M. A. Eckstein, *Toward a Science of Comparative Education*, Macmillan, London, 1969.

Nome, John, *Det Norske Misjonsselskaps Historie i Norsk Kirkelive*, vols. I and II, Dreyers Grafiske Anstalt, Stavanger, 1943.

Øidne, Gabriel, "Litt om Motsetninga Mellom Austlandet og Vestlandet," *Syn og Segn*, vol. 63, no. 3, 1957, pp. 97–114.

Østerud, Øyvind, *Agrarian Structure and Peasant Politics in Scandinavia*, Universitetsforlaget, Oslo, 1978.

Ousland, Godvin, *En Kirkehøvding: Professor Gisle Johnsen som Teolog og Kirkemann*, Lutherstiftelsens Forlag, Oslo, 1950.

Palstrøm, Henrik, "Om en befolkningsgruppes utvikling gjennom de siste 100 aar: Statistiske studier vedrørende norske akademikere," *Statsøkonomisk Tidsskrift*, 1935 (Oslo), pp. 161–370.

Perman, David, *Change and the Churches: An Anatomy of Religion in Britain*, The Bodley Head, London, 1977.

Pollan, Sonja, "Prestetradisjon og Presterekruttering, 1720–1955," *Tidsskrift for Samfunnsforskning*, vol. 3, 1962, pp. 83–98.

Pontoppidan, Erik, *Sannhet til Gudfryktighet*, Lutherstiftelsen, Oslo, 1964 [reissued in a modern Norwegian translation from the first edition; see title page: "Forklaring til Dr. Martin Luthers Lille Katekismus" Rettledining om alt det trenger og gjøre for aa bli salig].

Ramsfjell, Odd, *Kristendomsfaget i Folkeskolen: En historisk oversikt og en undersøking*, Magister Grad Avhandling, Oslo, 1960.

Repstad, Paal (ed.), *Det Religiøse Norge*, Gyldendal Norsk Forlag, Oslo, 1977.

Rokkan, Stein, "Norway: Numerical Democracy and Corporate Pluralism," in Robert A. Dahl (ed.), *Political Opposition in Western Democracies*, Yale University Press, New Haven and London, 1966, pp. 70–115.

"Geography, Religion, and Social Class: Cross Cutting Cleavages in Norwegian Politics," in S. M. Lipset and S. Rokkan (eds.), *Party Systems and Voter Alignments*, The Free Press, New York, 1967, pp. 363–403.

Rokkan, Stein and Henry Valen, "Regional Contrasts in Norwegian Politics," in E. Allardt and Y. Littunen (eds.), *Cleavages, Ideologies and Party Systems: Contributions to Comparative Political Sociology*, Transactions of the Westermarck Society, Helsinki, 1964, pp. 162–238.

Rudvin, Ola, *Den Kristelige Presse i Norge*, Lutherstiftelsens Forlag, Oslo, 1947.

Indremisjonsselskapets Historie, vol. I, *1868–1891*, vol. II, *1892–1968*, Lutherstiftelsens Forlag, Oslo, 1967 and 1970.

Rugge, Herman, "Almendannelsen," in *Norsk Kulturhistorie*, vol. IV, J. W. Cappelens Forlag, Oslo, 1940, p. 420.

Sandvik, Gudmund, *Prestegard og Prestelønn*, Universitetsforlaget, Oslo, 1965.

Sandvik, O. M., *Norsk Koralhistorie*, H. Aschehoug & Co., Oslo, 1930.

Seierstad, Andreas, *Kyrkjelegt Reformarbeid i Noreg Nittande Hundreaaret*, Bibliotheca Norwegiae Sacrae, II, A/S Lunde & Co. Forlag, Bergen, 1923.

Sejersted, Francis, *Den Vanskelige Frihet 1814–1851*, vol. X of *Norges Historie* (ed. Knut Mykland), J. W. Cappelens Forlag A. S., Oslo, 1978.

Semmingsen, Ingrid, "The Dissolution of Estate Society in Norway," *Scandinavian Economic History Review*, vol. 2, 1954, pp. 166–203.

Shaw, Joseph M., *Pulpit Under the Sky*, Augsburg Publishing House, Minneapolis, 1955.

Singer, Barnett, *Village Notables in Nineteenth Century France: Priests, Mayors, Schoolmasters*, State University of New York Press, Albany, New York, 1983.

Skappel, Simen, *Om Husmandsvaesenet i Norge*, Skrifter utgitt av Videnskapsselskapet i Kristiania, II Historisk-Filosofisk Klasse 2 Bind, Kristiania i Kommission Hos Jacob Dybwad, Christiania, 1922, pp. 1–192.

Hedmarkens AMT 1814–1914: En Fremstilling av Amtets Utvikling i de Forløpne Hundrede Aar utarbeidet til Norges Jubilaeumsutstilling 1914, Grøndahl & Søns, Kristiania, 1914.

Spilling, Gunnar, "Resultater av Kirketelling og Opinionsundersøkelser," *Kirke og Kultur*, vol. 62, 1957, pp. 385–399.

Stark, Werner, *The Sociology of Religion: A Study of Christendom*, vol. II, Fordham University Press, New York, 1967.

Steen, Sverre, *Det Gamla Samfunn*, J. W. Cappelen, Oslo, 1957.

Stinchcombe, Arthur L., *Theoretical Methods in Social History*, Academic Press, New York, 1978.

Stoeffler, F. Ernest, "Pietism," in Mircea Eliade (ed.), *The Encyclopedia of Religion*, Macmillan, New York, 1987, pp. 324–326.

Stone, Lawrence, "The Educational Revolution in England, 1560–1640," *Past and Present*, no. 28, 1964, pp. 41–80.

"Literacy and Education in England: 1640–1900," *Past and Present*, no. 42, Feb. 1969, pp. 69–139.

"Japan and England, A Comparative Study," reprinted in P. W. Musgrave (ed.), *Sociology, History and Education*, Methuen & Co., London, 1970.

Sundt, Eilert, *Om Giftermaal i Norge*, [first published 1866] Universitetsforlaget, Oslo, 1967.

Om Piperviken og Ruseløbakken: Undersøgelser om arbeidsklassens kaar og saeder i Christiania, Tidens Norsk Forlag, Oslo, 1968 [first published 1855].

Om Saedelighedstilstanden i Norge, vols. I and II, Pax Forlag, Oslo, 1968 [first published 1857].

Harham Et Eksempel fra fiskerdistrikterne, Universitetsforlaget, Oslo, 1971 [first published 1858–1859].

Tackett, Timothy, *Priest and Parish in Eighteenth-Century France: A Social and Political Study of the Curés in a Diocese of Dauphine, 1750–1791*, Princeton University Press, Princeton, 1977.

Tavuchis, Nicholas, *Pastors and Immigrants*, Nijhoff, The Hague, 1963.

Thyssen, A. Pontoppidan, "Danmark," in *Nordisk Historiker Møtet, I, Historiallinen Arkisto 62 utgiven av Finske Historiska Samfundet*, Helsinki, 1967, pp. 7–38.

Torgernsen, Ulf, "The Formation of Parties in Norway: The Problem of Right–Left Differences," *Scandinavian Political Studies*, vol. 2, Universitetsforlaget, Oslo, 1967, pp. 43–48.

The Market for Professional Manpower in Norway, Institute for Social Research, Oslo, 1967.

Church Independence and Doctrinal Purity, Institute for Social Research, Oslo, 1966.

Tveteraas, Harold L., *Norske Tidskrifter: Bibliografi over periodiske skrifter i Norge inntil 1920*, Universitetsbiblioteket, Oslo, 1940.

Valkner, Kristian, "Landstads og Hauges Salmebøker: Tiblivelseshistorie og Hymnologisk Karakteristikk," Norvegia Sacra, *Aarbok til Kunnskap om den Norske Kirke i Fortid og Samtid*, Tolvte Aargang, Steenske Forlag, Oslo, 1932.

Vaughan, Michalina and M. S. Archer, *Social Conflict and Educational Change in England and France: 1789–1848*, Cambridge University Press, Cambridge, 1971.

Wach, Joachim, *Sociology of Religion*, University of Chicago Press, Chicago, 1944.

Wallerstein, Immanuel, *The Modern World-System*, Academic Press, New York, 1974.

Weber, Max, "The Sociology of Religion," chapter 6 in Guenther Roth and Claus Wittich (eds.), *Economy and Society*, Bedminister Press, New York, 1968.

Wilson, Bryan R., *Religious Sects*, McGraw-Hill, New York, 1970.

Wisløff, Carl Fr., *Politikk og Kristendom* en studie omkring oppropet "Til Christendommens Venner i vort Land" (January 1883), A. S. Lunde & Co.'s Forlag, Bergen, 1961.

Wuthnow, Robert, "World Order and Religious Movements," in Albert Bergessen (ed.), *Studies of the Modern World System*, Academic Press, New York, 1980, pp. 57–75.

Wuthnow, Robert (ed.), *The Religious Dimension: New Directions in Quantitative Research*, Academic Press, New York, 1979.
Yinger, J. Milton, *The Scientific Study of Religion*, Macmillan, New York, 1970.
Zachariassen, Aksel, *Fra Marcus Thrane til Martin Tranmael*, Arbeidernes Opplysningsforbund, Oslo, 1962.

Bibliographic postscript:

As I was reading proofs (May 1989) of the present work the most recent issue of the *Scandinavian Journal of History* available in our library (vol. 11 no. 4 1986) came to my attention. It contains a fine review article by Bjørn Slettan: "Religious Movements in Norway. Attitudes and Trends in Recent Research." For those interested who read Norwegian a comparison of bibliographies will indicate what has not been included in my considerations.

Index

Other books in the series

J. Milton Yinger, Kiyoshi Ikeda, Frank Laycock, and Stephen J. Cutler: *Middle Start: An Experiment in the Educational Enrichment of Young Adolescents*

James A. Geschwender: *Class, Race, and Worker Insurgency: The League of Revolutionary Black Workers*

Paul Ritterband: *Education, Employment, and Migration: Israel in Comparative Perspective*

John Low-Beer: *Protest and Participation: The New Working Class in Italy*

Orrin E. Klapp: *Opening and Closing:Strategies of Information Adaptation in Society*

Rita James Simon: *Continuity and Change: A Study of Two Ethnic Communities in Israel*

Marshall B. Clinard: *Cities with Little Crime: The Case of Switzerland**

Steven T. Bossert: *Tasks and Social Relationships in Classrooms: A Study of Instructional Organization and Its Consequences*

Richard E. Johnson: *Juvenile Delinquency and Its Origins: An Integrated Theoretical Approach**

David R. Heise: *Understanding Events: Affect and the Construction of Social Action*

Ida Harper Simpson: *From Student to Nurse: A Longitudinal Study of Socialization*

Stephen P. Turner: *Sociological Explanation as Translation*

Janet W. Salaff: *Working Daughters of Hong Kong: Filial Piety or Power in the Family?*

Joseph Chamie: *Religion and Fertility: Arab Christian-Muslim Differentials*

William Friedland, Amy Barton, Robert Thomas: *Manufacturing Green Gold: Capital, Labor, and Technology in the Lettuce Industry*

Richard N. Adams: *Paradoxical Harvest: Energy and Explanation in British History, 1870–1914*

Mary F. Rogers: *Sociology, Ethnomethodology, and Experience: A Phenomenological Critique*

James R. Beniger: *Trafficking in Drug Users: Professional Exchange Networks in the Control of Deviance*

Andrew J. Weigert, J. Smith Teitge, and Dennis W. Teitge: *Society and Identity: Toward a Sociological Psychology*

Jon Miller: *Pathways in the Workplace: The Effects of Race and Gender on Access to Organizational Resources*

Michael A. Faia: *Dynamic Functionalism: Strategy and Tactics*

Joyce Rothschild and J. Allen Whitt: *The Co-operative Workplace: Potentials and Dilemmas of Organizational Democracy*

Russell Thornton: *We Shall Live Again: The 1870 and 1890 Ghost Dance Movements as Demographic Revitalization*

Severyn T. Bruyn: *The Field of Social Investment*

Guy E. Swanson: *Ego Defenses and the Legitimation of Behavior*

Liah Greenfeld: *Different Worlds: A Sociological Study of Taste, Choice and Success in Art*

* *Available from American Sociological Association, 1722, N Street, N.W., Washington, DC 20036*